The Tapestry

With Sermonettes In Rhyme

Hugh M. More

REDEMPTION PRESS

Published by Redemption Press, PO Box 427, Enumclaw, WA 98022.
Toll-Free (844) 2REDEEM (273-3336)

Redemption Press is honored to present this title in partnership with the author. The views expressed or implied in this work are those of the author. Redemption Press provides our imprint seal representing design excellence, creative content, and high-quality production.

The author has tried to recreate events, locales, and conversations from memories of them. In order to maintain their anonymity, in some instances the names of individuals, some identifying characteristics, and some details may have been changed, such as physical properties, occupations, and places of residence.

Cover design: Original water color art by our daughter, Manda K. Gorban.

ISBN 13: 978-1-64645-588-1 (Paperback)
978-1-951310-40-0 (ePub)

Library of Congress Catalog Card Number: 2022918622

Contents

Acknowledgments

When we read a dedication page at the front of a book, without exception we see listed people who have encouraged, strengthened, and supported us because they love us. I'm no exception to that truth—I've been blessed with more than my share of the kinds of people who encourage, especially my wife, Cilla, and also an especially important band of brothers, who for years encouraged me to put them together in a book. With that being said, I firmly believe that the Lord orchestrates even those whom he puts in our lives to help bring us to the place he wants us to be. As the Scripture verse says, "As iron sharpens iron, so one person sharpens another" (Proverbs 27:17 NIV). I have been extremely blessed.

It would be my greatest blessing that the Lord's fingerprints would be clearly seen in all these poems. He alone is the one who has been putting this whole project together from the beginning, starting some forty-six years ago. I have been blessed and honored to be the "pencil" that was allowed to put some words on paper that could hopefully encourage the reader to draw closer to the Lord. To God be all the praise and glory.

A special thanks to our daughter, Manda K. Gorban, for her original water-color artwork on the cover.

Introduction

Sermonettes? Whenever I've finished another poem, I've shared it with my wife, Cilla. If it happened to be a longer one, she'd make a lighthearted comment about the length. One day I responded with, "Well, if we ever do put the poems in a book, we can call it *Sermonettes in Rhyme*." Hence the subtitle.

Through the years, Cilla has told the story of my writing this way: "Early on there would be occasional poems—often short ones for scavenger hunts for our kids or a visit from the "Popcorn Fairy" for the kids across the street. My mom died in 1986, and Hugh wrote a poem for her called 'Where Did Mother Go?' Hugh's mom passed away in 2006, and he wrote one for her, too, called 'A Servant's Heart.' After that, a floodgate was opened up and many poems came."

Over the course of time, friends would encourage me to have some published, but I was hesitant for various reasons. As the years went by, the poems kept coming. It was a real blessing to be able to put some words together that meant something and might be an encouragement for someone. Any and all credit goes to the Lord, of course. I was blessed to just be a pencil. About a year ago, I hadn't written anything for some time, but in prayer I expressed my appreciation to the Lord for the blessing and asked, "If it be your will, I'd like to write some more poetry." I felt I heard the Lord respond with, "First, publish what you have." In hesitation, I put it on the back burner, did not follow through in obedience, and eventually forgot about it all together. Months later, I had the same conversation with the Lord and, not surprisingly, got the same response: "Publish." I know that God's timing is always perfect and that obedience is usually followed by confirmation. The joy of watching this project unfold has been phenomenal and very humbling. At this point, please let me encourage you—if the Lord is prompting you in some way, step out in faith and do it as the Lord leads. Through this whole experience the Lord has graciously revealed, as *The Tapestry* states in closing, everything in our lives is being or has been "Touched by the MASTER's hand."

The Tapestry

Every life is a tapestry, made up of many strands,
With each strand being carefully placed there by the Weaver's hands.
A color here, a texture there, at first won't look like much,
But as the pattern falls into place, reveals the Master's touch.
The colors need to change a lot to make this work of art.
The patterns in the Weaver's mind, known from the very start.
Some colors might come from testings; sometimes they're dyed thru pain.
Sometimes come from a mountain top; sometimes they're washed by rain.
Bright colors might be times of joy, dark colors from despair.
But as the Master picks each one, He handles it with care.
For each time a color changes, the two strands must be tied.
The knots are sometimes visible; sometimes they're meant to hide.
The special knot that joins each strand will never come undone.
The colors used will never fade, nor will they bleed or run.
For as each strand is put in place, that part is sanctified,
But when the work's at last revealed, it's all been glorified.
But here's the most amazing thing the Lord has helped refine,
That all the strands that make your life, are a small part of mine.
You see, no man is an island; that's not how we're designed.
Just as iron sharpens iron, by each we are refined.
We, too, often are impatient to see the "work" complete.
Each scene will finally be revealed when sitting at His feet.
So till the final knot is tied and all the ends are trim,
Trust in the fact the Weaver knows; what's best is known by Him.
You see, weaving is a process; the work's done strand by strand.
Found on completion of each work: "Touched by the Master's hand."

The Sounds of Amazing Grace

Ed and I had been friends for over thirty years and had developed a routine of getting together on Monday mornings for cribbage. More often than not, this time ended up in some kind of a Bible study or related discussion. On this particular morning, before I could sit down, Ed asked, "What are the sounds of amazing grace? We sang it yesterday. What are the sounds?" After some time in prayer and study, the Lord gave me two poems on the subject over the next few months—"The Sounds of Amazing Grace" and "More Sounds of Amazing Grace." I hope there will be more sounds added to the list.

Amazing grace, how sweet the sound.

Amazing grace, we often sing.
Have you heard yet the sounds that ring?
Combined, produce a harmony
We'll hear throughout eternity.
The sound that rings for all mankind;
Some will embrace and peace they'll find.
There will be some who turn deaf ears,
By their own choice be filled with fears.
The foll'wing list, though incomplete,
In eternity will be replete.
The first sound—silence—'twas no defense.
The courtroom scene was very tense.
Turned His cheek, no attempt to flee.
That sound expressed for you and me.
The next sound—hammer striking nail,
Imagined to the nth detail.
The sound of His vicar'ous pain
Is a part of the sweet refrain.
"Father, forgive," uttered with care.
Third sound heard—there's no judgment there.
By Jesus's blood, we've been washed clean.
The stain of sin will not be seen.
The fourth was uttered from the cross,

That sound that stops the sense of loss.
"It is finished!" 'Twas dark as night;
Helps us walk by faith, not by sight.
The next sound heard could not contrive
Before the women did arrive.
The crushing sound of rolling stone
Echoed a loud victor'ous tone.
The empty tomb, though, no sound heard;
Sensed sounds of vict'ry's promised word!
Produced the promise sought so long,
Resulting in redemption's song.
The story, at last, is now complete.
The sound of grace is very sweet.
Amazing grace, how sweet the sound.
No greater gift will e'er be found.

More of the Sounds of Grace

As was stated in an earlier poem, the list of those sounds is incomplete.
But there's one sound I'd like to add, because this sound will again repeat.

Amazement rattled heaven's gates as the angels watched God's plan unfold.
The rejoicing must have echoed loud when angels pushed and the stone
was rolled.

All those sounds mentioned just happened once salvation's work was
completely done
In those three days, when His blood was shed and brought the res'rection
of the Son.

But the sound I'm adding to the list, heard in God's presence around
the throne
'Tis the sound that all the angels make when another sinner has come home.

It's the sound they've made since time began, and they all respond as if
one voice.
Though each expression uniquely rings, 'tis harmony, for they all rejoice.

May that excitement be contagious, that our desire, too, would be the same.
To join together with the angels when another sinner calls His name.

That desire to see the lost redeemed, be the greatest drive within our soul.
That would make our Hallelujahs ring when a name is added to the roll.

Even as these words are being penned, there are more sounds that
come to mind.
There are two that will make a special sound when on that last day
they're combined.

The uniqueness of that sound we'll hear, that it's just a two-part harmony.
The first produced by wedding bells, then add rejoicing by you and me.

But till that day known by God alone, when the last redeemed will
heed the call.
Then the final sound that ends the list will echo throughout God's banquet hall.

From that day throughout eternity, that glorious sound will never fade.
And we'll forever be rejoicing for all the sounds amazing grace has made.

Jesus, God's grace that brought salvation, ordained to appear to all mankind.
Then obediently He provided that greatest gift we'll ever find.

But just one more thing before we go—we should live that sound in
every place.
Because we should know beyond a doubt that yes, we're surrounded by
His grace.

Amazing grace, oh, how sweet the sound.

A Part of My Story

"A Part of My Story" came from a men's retreat our church was having. We were singing an old chorus, "Abba Father, deep within my heart I cry." During that chorus, the Lord revealed his Fatherhood. I fell to my knees weeping and crying, "Oh, Daddy, Daddy, Daddy, thank you." I was able to share that with Mom, and we both had a good cry together.

Some years ago, when I was young, in three months I'd turn six.
My dad was sick and times were tough, knew we were in a fix.

Dad was sick 'cause his heart was weak; the valves no longer worked.
He had tried his best to provide; his duty he'd not shirk.

As time went on Dad's health grew worse; Mom knew the end was near.
What to do? And where would we go? The questions led to fear.

A single mom with two small kids, with heartaches—all alone,
More questions now than answers, not sure just who to phone.

But GOD who is always faithful stepped in to calm the fears,
And looking back, remember, His faithfulness through the years.

As years went by and I grew up, I struggled with a fear;
How good a father could I be, 'cause mine was never near?

Again, GOD in His faithfulness, His timing was just right,
Revealed His promised Fatherhood; He'd just been out of sight.

The years of fear that I had known just melted on the floor.
I knew the load I'd carried would be a load no more.

Who could find a better model than He who made the mold?
The answer is not far away; our hand He wants to hold.

He brought to mind the Scriptures, spoke of His Father's heart;
And how He'd held me in HIS arms right from the very start.

There are still times I question how good a dad I've been,
But knowing GOD's grace will cover, I'll be at peace again.

I know there's been some things I done they've needed to forgive,
But even those mistakes have worth; those acts can help them live.

I know your story 'twill differ; the facts won't be the same.
But if your heart's been broken, please stop—call out His name.

Know your call won't go unanswered; He knows your troubled heart.
He's standing by to help you, to help your healing start.

As the truths that He has promised take root within your heart,
Troubles will start to melt away; the peace you've sought will start.

The Father of the fatherless has called to us by name,
And longs to hear us call to Him by a very special name . . . "ABBA."

Encouragement

Fear Defeated

When the trials of life surround us and we know we're in the fight,
Firmly dressed up in God's armor, with your shield, do not take flight.

Standing firm in God's convictions causes foes to stand and doubt.
They will always be bewildered, for His will works all things out.

Don't be frightened by opponents, those who mock at you and sneer.
The courage of your convictions will tell them their end is near.

You don't need to fear destruction; you'll be saved and that by God.
He's promised to never leave you as you walk this earthen sod.

The thing that causes them to fear, even though they don't know why;
The God who made the universe is not threatened when they lie.

He knows that there will come the day each and every knee will bow.
Not threatened by man's arrogance, He shows patience for right now.

As we stand in the conviction that God's plans can never fail,
The fear that brings defeat to us always comes to no avail.

The Scriptures tell us not to fear, to be trusting in His care.
For when the Lord is on our side, our enemies need beware.

He's never given any trial without power to get through.
His pledge is in His written word, and you know my friend, it's true.

First John One

Don't try to ignore or cover it up.
Instead, bring it into the light.
To simply ignore it won't change a thing.
Confession will make it all right.

John's first letter tells in one verse nine,
Confession is good for the soul.
When we shed the light on sins we've committed,
A rightness returns to our soul.

With all our rough edges, failures, and flaws,
Our Father created a way
To wipe the slate clean and start once again
In fellowship, day after day.

How many times have we knelt down in prayer
And said, "Lord, I've done it again."
The response that comes back time after time,
"You've confessed—there is no 'again.'

"When you come to Me to seek forgiveness,
I will forever do what's best;
Your sins will be placed as far as can be,
As far as the east is from west.

"Because of the cross, you've been justified,
If you will but ask and believe.
Now by believing you've been forgiven,
All you have to do is receive."

For His Glory

We've been created in His image.
Not just to show His craftsmanship,
His purpose, desire, and reason;
He desires man's fellowship.
A people for His own possession,
And that with a goal in mind,
Proclaiming to the world His glory,
How He's treated us so kind.
To boldly speak of His mighty acts
And exclaiming all His worth,
And so bringing forth praise and glory from
Every creature here on earth.
In His Word, God says He's jealous,
That His glory be revealed.
His glory to be shouted far and wide,
That the truth not be concealed.
So with this singleness of purpose,
Double minded He is not.
It appears that's the ultimate goal,
That His glory would be sought.
He's not being egotistical
To desire His glory known.
It's because He knows how we'll respond,
When we see His glory shown.
So you see, it's just His heart of love
He's expressed toward all mankind.
That sign above Him could have read,
"Greatest love you'll ever find."

Galatians, We're Free

Galatians tells us that we've been set free
And don't be shackled in bonds of slavery.

Keeping the law while we're running the race,
We'll find that we are not living by grace.

To live by the law, we can't miss at all;
To miss just one law you're guilty of all.

Our efforts are wasted, the price has been paid;
All of our troubles on Jesus were laid.

"Harken, my children, you've been justified;
Conditions were met the day Jesus died.

"It's over, it's finished, just as He said;
To the law of slavery you can be dead."

The chains have been broken; you are now free,
Walking by faith you can live righteously.

God Provides

We say that we trust you
In all that we do;
Your hand is upon us
And guiding us thru.

But as we face the end
Of our active days
And can no longer work
To make our own way,

We struggle and worry
And fail to abide
And forget the promise
That you will provide.

We have said, "It's your hand
That helps us make wealth,"
But with those days fading,
We count on that wealth.

When we look to that wealth
That we've set aside,
We trust in that money
And fail to abide.

God, you have promised us
You'll meet all our needs,
Like the birds of the air
That you always feed.

If we but trust you
Through all of our days,
We'll not have to worry;
You'll guide all our ways.

God's Museum

We like to build museums, showing off things man has made,
And spend a lot of money just to put them on parade.

If we could put them end to end, it would be quite a show.
But it wouldn't take a lifetime if to each one we would go.

We get so proud and arrogant and get puffed up with pride,
To marvel at the works of man and all the things we've tried.

Of all we've done and things we've made, the list is really short
Compared to God's museum, where we see a full report.

"God's Museum" is the universe, stretches on, will never end,
Filled with things that God has made; it's there for us my friend,

To ponder and to wonder at how this came to be,
To see it all and understand will take eternity.

To marvel at the mountains or an eagle on the wing,
An honest heart would have no choice but to rejoice and sing.

The wonder of His handiworks, as great as they may be,
Pales in the comparison of His love for you and me.

By God's own admission, the greatest work He's ever done
Was make our human likeness in the image of His Son.

Although we are His works of art, the works not finished yet,
He just keeps on changing us—don't you see, the paint's still wet?

But even though there's work to do to finish up His plan,
We were created for good works to serve our fellow man.

When love serves one another, then it's plain for all to see
That Jesus died to save us and to set each captive free.

God's Word Is Final

Let God's Word be true and every man a liar,
Yet we still ask His approval to play with fire.

His Word gives us wisdom for the pathway of life;
Ignoring that wisdom brings nothing but strife.

The self-will of life will always get in the way,
Looking for an out, rather than trust and obey.

We pray asking the Lord for our wants to be so,
When God's Word already tells us which way to go.

The arrogance to ask the Creator to change,
To alter His ways and for my life rearrange.

Quickly humble yourself and get down off the throne
By repenting of the pride to which we're all prone.

He will not give His blessing to go your own way,
His words that are spoken forever will stay.

There'll be no arbitration, no room for appeal.
God's Word's always final, and He won't make a deal.

If God's Word's not final and each goes his own way,
Then God is not Lord, and rebellion rules the day.

So flee from the temptation to seek your own way,
And avoid the appearance that could lead you astray.

He Gives Us Grace

Just because He gives us grace,
We think we're off the hook.
We no longer need obedience
Once we are written in the book.

We try to get away with things
That we really should not do,
Thus imposing on His grace
And think we'll make it through.

If that's your line of thinking,
You just don't understand.
God's grace not meant to be abused;
It is there helping us to stand.

Just because He gives us grace,
It's not to be misused.
The gift is free, should never
For the gain of self be used.

Obedience, not based on works,
Is what we get to do.
Works express a thankful heart,
'Cause it's love calling us to do.

When God's Word says "If you love me,
Do what I ask of you."
Not referring to the law
But daily tasks for us to do.

Out of love and a thankful heart,
Our tasks should all be done.
Not for profit that we might gain,
But live the image of the Son.

Holding On

"We must hold on," we're often told.
To pass the test—refined like gold.
Encouraged then to persevere,
It's then our hope can be brought near.
The process will at times be tough;
Wonder if we'll be strong enough.
Spend time in prayer to ask for aide,
Because we're sure our strength will fade.
Our fingernails are getting weak;
The knotted rope we truly seek.
We seek for things to stop the slide
To find that thing—peace will abide.
Can find that hope begins to fade;
Forget the promises God has made.
When troubles come, seems faith would fail.
We oft forget this one detail.
It's not our strength that helps us stand;
It's only His almighty hand.
His word more than a time or two
Says He will not abandon you.
The question, then, is very clear.
Which posture does away with fear?
By hanging to the final strands,
Or resting in His loving hands?

I Do, But I Don't

The war goes on this side of the grave—
Of the two laws, which one will I crave?
The law of God my mind wants to do,
The law of the flesh too oft choose to do.
The struggle goes on day after day;
My desire is to walk the right way.
Desire and action, oft far apart,
The battle still rages deep in my heart.
That which I want I don't always do;
That which I don't too often do.
The good that I wish I do not do,
Practicing sin I don't wish to do.
The struggle runs deep. Who'll set us free?
Thanks be to God, thru Jesus we're free.
We're no longer slaves to be bound by sin;
We've been set free from death due to sin.
Walking in Christ we won't be condemned.
We've been set free even though we've sinned.
Freedom to serve in newness of life.
Walk in victory, a Spirit-led life.
So give thanks again—God set us free;
Jesus provided for life on that tree.

Integrity

When we're all alone and no one's around,
Then a true test of our hearts can be found.

At times like this, it's just God and "me,"
A real true test of our integrity.

When we're all alone and nothing's an act,
Actions revealing leaves nothing but fact.

As to the condition that our heart's in,
Will we yield to the temptation of sin?

We can abuse grace and say that's okay;
God will forgive, and I'll go my own way.

Or do we hold fast and turn sin aside,
With ever in mind our goal "to abide."

Behavior can change to make self look good,
But just changing behavior does us no good.

We know and God knows just what's deep within;
Compromised behavior's nothing but sin.

As God's given conscience, the Spirit's our guide,
To lead and to guide and help us abide.

When we walk clean, then sin loses its hold,
Walking in confidence we can be bold.

Boldly approaching the throne by God's grace,
We will be able to behold His face.

Our Struggles and Hopes Can Lead to Life—Theirs

In the midst of a struggle, often hard to keep in mind
That all things work out for our good and true peace we can find.
Though all seems grim and troubles rise and we see no end in sight,
Sometimes hard to remember to keep our focus in the fight.
Those struggles have a purpose; they'll teach us how to cope.
Testings bring perseverance, and perseverance leads to hope.
So when the bottom that you're looking for is seen by looking up,
Please don't become discouraged or ever think of giving up.
The One who hung the stars in place and knows each one by name
Also knew us in our mother's womb before we got our name.
He chose the color of our hair and knew just how tall we'd be.
Fearfully and wonderfully made for all the world to see.
He knows everything about us and just what we're going through
And has all the grace we'll ever need to help us see it thru.
Circumstances that we deal with, not at random or by chance,
They're all a part of God's design, that our faith would be enhanced,
For tested faith adds perseverance—that completed—more mature,
And then not lacking anything, God gets the glory, that's for sure.
Brother James gave us instructions as to how the process starts.
It all begins when we express all faith's joy that's in our hearts.
For that joy expressed through trusting might show them that it's worthwhile,
For them to trust the God we serve and give them reason, too, to smile.
When they see a faith unshakable, that's as solid as a rock,
They'll know that something's diff'rent and hopefully they'll take stock—
The stock of noticed diff'rence between our life and theirs,
And that they'd desire to trust the One on whom we've cast our cares.
When they see that we're not frightened by troubles that we face,
They will know that something's missing and that we've been
touched by grace.
It could just be our action that gives the final nudge,

That they, too, realize God wants to be their Savior, not their judge.
So remember that they're watching after everything we do,
To see if by the way we live, is our testimony true?
Because when there's no difference between our words and deeds,
Objections begin to crumble; that's the time for planting seeds,
Because the "true life" they've observed is tilling fallow ground.
And will accept those planted seeds that new life will abound.
So don't be dismayed when struggles come that try to cause you strife.
They just might be the witness they need to choose eternal life.

Patience

We seem to ask for patience
When burdened down with stress,
Always looking for an out
Each time we face a test.

But patience is not given;
It only comes thru tests,
But it's those "awful" trials
That help us know God's best.

Though patience is a virtue
That everybody seeks,
'Tis gifting of the Spirit
That our behavior tweaks.

We all want to be patient;
Deep down we know it's right.
But when my "self" gets challenged,
It usually starts a fight.

The fight goes on within us,
To see which will, will win
Each time I defend my will,
God says that it is sin.

No matter what the battle,
It boils down to trust.
In fact, if God is in control,
trusting is a must.

Patience speaks of trusting
No matter what the test.
Trusting in the God who cares
will bring us peace and rest.

Perseverance, a Good Thing

James speaks of our perseverance and just how it must run its course.
That through the trials and testings, we become an effective force.
That force can cause the world to see there's a way of life that's better.
The keys to which are always found written in God's holy letter.
James states it's when we persevere we'll get the strength to help us stand.
With the amazing and full awareness that strength comes from His hand.
It's not by works that we can do to gain the strength to run the race.
Even faith for perseverance will come by His amazing grace.
It's through those trials and tests, my friend, that God says we're sanctified.
Then the next step in the process, we will someday be glorified.
Another thing that's wrought within, we'll find a total sense of peace;
And from the daily stress of life God will provide a sweet release.
That release is not deliverance that there'll be no more tests
But that you can face each trial with an attitude of rest.
Sometimes when faced with trials and tests, our first response can be despair.
We struggle with the strife it brings, can be convinced God doesn't care.
Then Paul chimes in in Romans, tells us, "In suff'ring to rejoice."
Which will precede perseverance, thru our expression made by choice.
Perseverance builds character, and then character leads to hope.
And hope will never disappoint, our source of strength with which to cope.
The promise of the "Crown of Life" to those by choice who seek His face
And rest in the confirmation, proclaimed by His "Amazing Grace."
Though the "Crown of Life" we're given speaks of rewards eternally,
It also speaks of current gifts, those experienced by you and me.
We often think eternity is an era far away,
That starts the day that this flesh dies, but it's as current as today.
We are eternal beings. That means forever without end.
The question, then, when life is o'er—Where in eternity will you spend?

Pure Joy?

Do we count it pure joy
when facing a trial,
or are we complaining
behind a big smile?

God says, "I've planned this."
And we're wondering why.
He says, "You'll know why
some sweet by-and-by."

"You really need patience
for to become mature,
not lacking in anything,
so your heart can be pure."

"You all want fast answers.
You're not trusting to wait.
You put all your efforts
in controlling your fate."

I've asked you to trust me
without any doubt.
Doubting will cause you to
be tossed about."

"Tossed about by the wind
and by waves tossed about,
will happen to you if
you live with much doubt."

There's no room for doubt
in lives built on faith,
when trusting in Jesus,
the Lord of our faith.

So put all your trust
in Jesus, "The Rock."
Your foundation is sure
when built on that "Rock."

Riches and Kindness

Why do we miss "It's His riches and kindness"
that draws us away to himself?
We overlook His patient forbearance
and work hard to earn it ourselves.

We take it so lightly, not hearing His words,
and still try to go our own way.
The more we try, we're deeper in debt,
to earn our salvation—no way.

We take it so lightly in other ways too,
by our not showing to others
patience and kindness Christ's given us—
need to start giving to others.

If that's the case, then we just don't understand.
We show that we are ungrateful,
Receiving so much and not give it back,
No way of showing we're thankful.

Start putting into practice what's been done to you,
Stop showing your hardness of heart.
Patience and kindness given others
Presents to them our Savior's heart.

When We're Tested

We all like special treatment
when trials come our way.
Our choice would be for comfort
and to take the pain away.

When trials or a struggle
invade our quiet life,
what's our very first response
when we're troubled by some strife?

We usually seek deliverance
instead of taking time
to ask for conformation,
"Lord, what's your will this time?"

Can we trust this God of love?
Trust that He knows what's best?
And thru the process trusting
we can walk in perfect rest.

Each trial has a purpose;
they're never just for spite.
The purpose is a process;
"Lord, please help me see things right."

Trials come to make us strong
and learn to walk by faith.
Hear Him say, "Well done, my child,"
when we behold His face.

Trust in the One Who Cares

So deep in depression that you're lost in despair,
knowing that nobody cares.
Troubled and tormented to the point of defeat,
knowing that nobody cares.
Completely immobile without motivation,
knowing that nobody cares.
Is believing a lie the start of the problem?
Thinking that nobody cares.
Caught up in our problems, we can get discouraged,
thinking that nobody cares.
If we just had someone to tell all our troubles,
wishing for someone who cares.
Be encouraged, my friend. Your solution's at hand;
I know Someone who cares.
We've got many stories of some saints gone before.
They knew the One who cares.
And because they knew Him, they could face their troubles
and trust in the One who cares.
Why would two brothers be singing at midnight?
They trusted the One who cares.
And Job was yet another so afflicted and troubled
yet trusted the One who cares.
Through all of their troubles they rejoiced and gave thanks.
They knew of the One who cares.
As we trust in the Lord with a thankful heart,
peace comes from the One who cares.
It may not be easy to see through the darkness
and to see the One who cares.
Take heart then, my friend. It is time to begin
to trust in the One who cares.

So never give up and believe it won't happen.
Please trust in the One who cares.
We can look at our sorrows, forgetting the promise,
Not trusting the One who cares.
Believe no more lying that comes straight from satan;
Learn to trust the One who cares.
Snuggle under His wing or climb up in His lap,
And rest in the One who cares.
"I'll never leave nor forsake during your troubles!"
A quote from the One who cares.
In the midst of your troubles, He's calling to you;
He wants you to know He cares.
In case nobody's told you, or you just forgot,
Jesus is the One who cares.

Today

Let's put in perspective
what we call "Today";
in some ways it doesn't exist.

Today as we know it
is not very long;
passing so quickly,
it seems like a blur.
In some ways it doesn't exist.

The moment we see it,
it's already gone.
Before I can say it,
it is yesterday.
In some ways it doesn't exist.

Before it can get here,
we call it tomorrow.
I can't change what's coming
nor know what's coming.
In some ways it doesn't exist.

One equals a thousand;
a thou equals one.
If morning starts today,
full of God's grace,
in some ways it never ends.

Unlimited mercy,
unlimited grace.
His love is so boundless,
grace without measure.
I'm glad today never ends.

So get close to Calvary,
get close to the cross,
taste the endless love of God!
And enjoy the moment.
I'm glad that it never ends!

Thru It All

He came not just to set me free
from all the storms of life,
removing all the problems
I'm fraught with in this life.

Too often when I look at life,
I grumble and complain;
ask God, "Why'd you treat me so?"
I just don't like the pain.

I want life really easy
and never have much strife.
My comfort level's shaken,
just want a quiet life.

But the Scriptures say much different.
my problems will be real,
and will have many struggles
to keep an even keel.

Every pain that comes in life
intended for my good.
Hard to keep that fact in sight;
can pain be for my good?

It's not the pain that's good for me,
it's what it brings about;
causes me to trust in Him.
He will work all things out.

Sometimes we won't understand
the value of a test.
The answer's in eternity;
we'll then know what was best.

They're Watching

The world is looking for ways to find peace,
To ease their troubles and find sweet release.
If we don't show them a new way of life,
Then they have no hope of ending their strife.
The world is watching to see if it's real,
This life called "Christian"—where is the appeal?
Our claim that Christ will make everything right,
They watch to see how we stand in the fight.
We all have struggles and things we must face;
We should act diff'rent, surrounded by grace.
If turmoils and struggles don't steal our peace,
'Twill show them the way to that much-sought release.
If you claim Christ, then your life's on parade;
World looks hard to see the difference it made.
When in "your" storm and your life is a mess,
Then where is this God who says he will bless?
They look at statistics, mocking our claim.
So much for God's power; stats are the same.
Where is this power you're trying to sell?
Show me, that I, too, the vict'ry may tell.
So let's live a changed life, one full of peace;
To witness this change, all arguments cease.
There must be a reason. How can it be?
The peace that you have, I want it for me.

The Lord Is Near

I feel like despair has finally set in.
I cry out, "O God!" again and again.
I cry all day long, by night, still no rest.
My eyes fill with tears; hope it's just a test.
I feel so forsaken, so all alone.
Is this punishment, my sins to atone?
I've read your promises—"I'll make a way,"
But here I still struggle day after day.
Heaven seems to be as solid as brass;
Seems so foreboding, my prayers just won't pass.
Starting to question, "What is it I've done
To cause this silence?" Response? There's just none.
I've prayed and I've fasted, seeking your face,
In danger of stumbling, losing the race.
My strength is waning; I'm ready to fall,
Tempted to doubt that you're listening at all.
Exhausted, I stopped, no strength left to stand.
'Twas then that I felt the touch of your hand.
Quickly I turned; I could not see your face.
Overwhelmed, I'd been touched by Amazing Grace.
Though nothing's yet changed, your peace is in place;
Your promise is here—I'm enabled by grace!
That calm assurance that you'll make a way
Gives me the vict'ry o'er struggles each day.
To know that you're there is more than enough
To cause vict'ry to rise when life gets tough.
Yet there will be times I'll struggle with fear,
Until I recall that you, Lord, are near.
Remember the footprints left in the sand?
'Twas your love that carried when I couldn't stand.
or
My piggyback ride when I couldn't stand.

The Banquet

Every time the Word is open,
My friend, it's a virtual feast.
Yet we leave the table hungry
'cause we settle for the least.

The whole table's set before us,
But yet we still pick and choose.
Instead of being blessed by all,
Pick just what we want to use.

If it's not just what we desired,
Think we've heard it all before,
We'll often turn our hearing off,
Then worship becomes a chore.

If we choose not to hear what's said
'cause we have our boundaries set,
Then we're rejecting what God planned;
We have not surrendered yet.

My friend, God has ordained the words
That He'd have for us each day,
So please don't close your heart and mind;
Hear all that He has to say.

God's Word is always given us,
And should come as no surprise,
He wants us to pay attention
So He can open up our eyes.

To choose the things we're blinded to,
Which by nature we can't see,
That will stop the world from seeing
Jesus glorified in me.

Take a Break

Stop for just a moment, friend,
and think about the state you're in.
Justified, no longer bound
to a life where sin abounds.
By His grace you were set free
when Christ died upon that tree.
Paid the price for one and all
to redeem us from the fall.
Mastery of sin was broken;
freedom now's not a token.
Freedom's key is to believe
the blood of Christ sins to relieve.
Just because we've been set free,
cannot do what pleases "me."
Should not give our lives to sin,
just to see God's grace again.
No, my friend, should not be so;
back to sin we should not go.
Since to sin no longer bound,
freedom now in Christ is found.

Sin versus Surrender

We hear great testimonies and just don't realize,
Sin has consequences, not dependent on their size.

Each of us will take the test; the question is the same.
Have you called on Jesus Christ and trusted in His name?

Some will say, "I'm not that bad; I've done a lot of good.
That should get my ticket punched; I really think it should."

Others say, "I'm really bad; just look at what I've done.
Here's a list of where I failed; it just can't be undone."

There is an understanding that we must earn our pass
And work our way toward heaven and not be second class.

The One who wrote the rule book has said, "It isn't so.
It's not by the works you do but by the love you show."

The first love's to the Master, Creator of All Things;
He who set the stars in place and is the King of Kings.

The next words out of Jesus's mouth: "Must love your fellow man."
Put the two together to complete the Savior's plan.

Both loves shown in surrender, by giving up my will,
To have the final right to say in whose will I fulfill.

You can argue if you want and try to make your case.
All the works that you have done won't help you win the race.

God says the way to heaven is not by what you do.
The only way to get there's by what's been done for you.

Jesus made the sacrifice; He paid for you and me.
His blood shed upon the cross was spilled to set us free.

Life Can Be Difficult

This life can be difficult,
With hardship and trials.
At times we're not happy
And can struggle with denial.

The continuous hardships
That just seem to go on,
And with no end in sight
Then all our hoping seems gone.

Your body may be broken
And your life racked with pain;
Spirit close to breaking,
Our cry: "Please, Lord, not again."

When all our hoping seems lost
And we're losing our grip,
Then take courage, my friend—
Life is really a short trip.

This, too, shall soon be passing;
Our life's but a vapor.
Your troubles shall vanish
Like a match to some paper.

God tells us our afflictions,
Momentary and light,
Yet don't seem so easy
In the middle of the fight.

In the middle of the trial,
Think we're failing the test.
Then be patient, my friend.
You're preparing for the best.

That one day 'twill soon happen,
In the blink of an eye
Troubles will be over;
Hope there is time for goodbyes.

Don't forget, then, my dear one,
In the midst of the pain,
The Lord will never leave you;
Praise finds His presence again.

Sanctified

Sanctified, sanctified, what can we do,
even the will to obey comes from you.
We're told, work it out with trembling and fear,
but even our works won't draw Jesus near.

It's not by acts or works we have done.
It's only because of the true Righteous One
that we are seen spotless and able to stand,
gently led by His great loving hand.

The works that we do show our devotion
to the One who set the plan in motion.
If the works are done to gain a reward,
honor and glory won't go to the Lord.

Sanctification, the process in life,
proving salvation is making new life.
The only way we can truly obey
is pick up our cross and die every day.

Dying to self—such a hard thing to do—
will only happen as Jesus helps you.
Pride wants to say that we earned our own way,
and that's why we struggle day after day.

"Come to me and rest," the Father has said.
"The work's been completed; you've nothing to dread.
My grace makes it free; you've no more to do.
Salvation's gift ends the struggle for you."

Our labor is only to enter His rest,
a willing vessel will pass every test.
Sanctified by the grace that's been given,
the sanctified saints are bound for heaven.

Short of the Glory

We all fall short of the glory of God,
not a matter of how close or how far.
The issue is that we just can't make it,
no matter how far we are up on the bar.

How great a sin is just doesn't matter.
The issue is not how big or how small.
We like to rate from the worst to the least;
if we've broken one, we're guilty of all.

Our nature's corrupted, polluted by sin.
We just can't go back to the garden again,
Back to the garden, in fellowship sweet,
walking and talking just like that again.

The standard's been set; it's called perfection.
Only one person lived up to the test.
Because Jesus passed, the score goes to us.
Only believe—it's a one-question test.

There's no work involved in order to pass.
First step toward completion: answer the call.
If we're not called, we won't get the answer.
Just believing in Jesus, He paid it all.

The Image of God

The image of God so holy and just,
majestic beyond compare.
Without our hearts being touched by the Spirit,
we're totally unaware.

Who can fathom the expanse of His awe
and still be able to stand?
Yet at the same time surrounded by grace,
be touched by His loving hand.

The God who created the stars in space
and everything else we see
has stated emphatically o'er and o'er
His great love for you and me.

We all want a God who meets all our needs,
but please, oh please, understand,
it's not about you, it's not about me.
He guides with a loving hand.

He cares for and loves us, yet at the same time
the requirement's still the same.
We have to be righteous and totally clean
if we want to bear His Name.

It's not by our works or efforts we make
to help us bear that Name.
Jesus did it all, and He paid the price;
He bore the cross and the shame.

He paid the price for the sins we have done,
on the cross with all its shame.
Salvations's a gift that's open to all;
we're blessed by His righteous Name.

The Truth Within

Every man's without exception, for the truth that lies within;
each is held accountable for the truth God placed therein.

God says, "There's no exceptions; you can see it every hour,
because what's been created reveals my eternal power."

Even more than power shown, divine nature's plain to see.
Nature held by God alone, plainly there for all to see.

Heavens declare His glory, the earth proclaims His works.
Day and night proclaiming truths clearly seen in all His works.

Called "Natural Revelation," God gives us the evidence.
Everything that has been made covered with His fingerprints.

We have to be more honest. It's not that we cannot see;
the truth is we don't want to; no excuse for you and me.

Turning eyes away from God will not stop that He is real.
He's still God, will always be; doesn't matter how we feel.

We exchange the truth of God, the truth that God has placed within,
exchanged that truth for the lie, thus committing mortal sin.

The truth that we're so quick to trade, denying that there's a God.
I choose to walk my own way, saying, "I will be my God."

Life's fraught with tribulation and sometimes peace within.
Whether it be peace or strife, the Lord's truth's where we begin.

Just one way to break the grip of the self-will's powerful force.
Humbly trust the living God; He will guide you thru life's course.

Victories Won

We all have heard stories
of victories won.
The victories are over
the things we have done.

We stumble and we fall
and struggle with grief,
but Jesus has told us,
"Trust Me for relief."

The greatest of stories
that we'll ever tell
are ones of the moments
when we never fell.

It's so little for Jesus
to pick us back up.
The story's still stronger;
He helped us stand up.

But don't ever make light
of victories won.
They all come about
by grace from the Son.

So please make it your goal—
try not to stumble.
Give glory to God.
He'll help you be humble.

Your grace is sufficient,
and it is so true,
when we walk in grace,
we'll be just like you.

We all need to hear more
of "He helped me stand"
by making the choice
to hold Jesus's hand.

If we hold Jesus's hand
and never let go,
then as we obey,
His glory will show.

Strength thru Trials

In the midst of a trial and can only see pain,
We're not looking forward to the strength we might gain.

The strength gained by testing we would rather not face;
It's our ease and comfort we'd much rather embrace.

But God says, "It's thru testing your strength will increase;
Every time it is proof that My love will not cease."

When we're going thru trials, God gives us a choice
In the midst of those trials we must learn to rejoice.

With strength as it grows, it builds character next.
To character add hope; it's all there in the text.

When our hope is in Christ, it will not disappoint;
As we walk thru a trial the Spirit will anoint.

When that strength is received thru the trials of life,
Our hearts get encouraged, and we'll have much less strife.

My friend, be forewarned, for more strife there will be.
It just will not have the same effect upon "me."

In the midst of our trials, we'll find we're at rest,
Brings glory to God, cause we know, He knows what's best.

Faith

Faith Delivered

Although faith was delivered once to us all,
That day on the cross, the day Christ took our fall.
Our faith seems to waver; sometimes we fight with doubt.
We'd rather not wait to see how things work out.
Oh how I wish it were at once a done deal;
Faith given in total at our first appeal.
But God in His wisdom desires it to grow
The strength of our faith to others will show.
We've faith for the moment; the promise is clear.
"I will never leave you—I'll always be near."
Whenever we're tested, he'll give a way out.
The choice, though, is ours to just trust and not doubt.
The object of faith is where the strength lies.
It's not what I feel or what's seen thru my eyes.
It's by the words that I speak, pleasing to me,
That God has to react, right? Let's wait and see.
"Lord, here's the verse; now you must do as you say."
I'd fall on my knees if I acted that way.
How arrogant of us to tell God what's His will.
Our desire should be His will to fulfill.
Since He's the Creator, how dare we presume
That our will is greater, commands the throne room?
Instead let's give thanks He provides for His will,
Learning to trust Him, His will to fulfill.
Faith cometh by hearing, so yes, it's a test;
By waiting on God, we'll know we've been blessed.
Faith given by measure is always just right.
God knows what we need to stand in the fight.

Faith of the Mustard Seed

The faith of the mustard seed, taught far and wide—
It is not the seed's size that makes faith abide.
It is not faith that's little, that brings things about;
It is just faith in God when we do not doubt.
The faith of the mustard seed knows that it knows
That God's predetermined the way that it grows.
That there's naught that can happen to alter that fact;
'Twas preordained by God how the seed would react.
It will not be a peach tree, a plum or a fig;
In fact, it knows that it won't be that big.
Yet just big enough for birds to feather their nest
And stop for a moment in cool shade to rest.
It won't do anything but what God has designed;
To God's perfect will it's forever resigned.
That little seed knows, when controlled by God's hand,
That nothing can alter the things God has planned.
The faith given by measure is always enough.
It will give us the strength to deal with life's "stuff."
So the choice then is ours to believe or to doubt
That God, by His grace, will work everything out.
Now with total confidence and no fear at all,
Know God will sustain you and won't let you fall.
In fact, when we live our life and know that we know,
Then God's gifting of faith to others will show.

Faith versus Works

Such a battle about faith and works.
The battle goes on and on.
Some say it's faith, and some say it's works
Salvation's dependent on.

Look in the book and read what it says,
Then change the thoughts of your mind.
James said it well—it's not either/or;
It's working and faith combined.

Ephesians 2 makes it quite clear,
It's not our works that save us,
That our works are actually evidence
That God has already saved us.

Romans is strong; we are saved by faith,
By God's grace we're justified.
Paul says it again; we're saved by faith,
By works we are sanctified.

Galatians speaks of our being free
From the law of death and sin,
Not to be caught in bondage again,
And walk with freedom within.

Glorious grace by which we are saved,
Works, proof of a living faith,
Labors of love out of gratitude
Perfecting the life of faith.

Thoughts on Faith

God asked Abraham to trust Him and leave his Father's land.
Go to a place he knew not of, be led there by God's hand.
His trek began with his first step; God gave "no end in sight."
But Abraham stepped out in faith that God would do things right.
When God had fulfilled His promise, giving Canaan as his home,
Told him to walk throughout the land, and that he'd ne'er more roam.
But then another promise came, that he would have a son.
That even though advanced in years, he'd be the promised one.
Though God didn't give a promised date, still Abraham believed,
Counted to him as righteousness, by faith he had received.
The promise did not come quickly; in fact he had to wait.
The Bible says 'twas twenty plus; his wife said, "It's too late."
But God proved Himself as faithful; Sarah at last conceived.
She faithful now considered God, and now she, too believed.
Today we're given promises, the quiz, "Do you believe?"
Before we see the completion, by faith, do we receive?
We're asked to walk by faith alone and not to walk by sight.
The things now seen will one day fade, and then we'll see things right.
Too often we get impatient; we just don't want to wait,
But God's timing's always perfect—He's not been one minute late.
The reason we're impatient, by time we are constrained.
But God will never be controlled; God's will, will be retained.
If we desire to please the Lord, then faith must be our walk.
Then the peace that comes from trusting speaks louder than our talk.
True faith is like a three-legged stool that needs all three to stand;
The perfect balance of all three held firmly by Their hand.
The first leg is to know God's will; the second is to believe.
The third is then to trust in God; true faith we will receive.
Let's think of it another way. Each leg can represent
Functions of the Triune God that never will relent.

God's ways are always perfect; sometimes we don't agree.
The thing that causes all our grief, the future we cannot see.
A life by faith is a process, with progress day by day.
As we daily learn to trust Him, He will provide a way.
It's like those wondrous tapestries that are made strand by strand;
Displayed on each completed work, "Stitched by the Master's hand."
Those tapestries line the hallway as trophies of His grace.
When the gall'ry is completed, each has a special place.
That hallway won't be cluttered; there's nothing out of place.
The banner o'er the entrance, "Touched by His Amazing Grace."

Prayer

Did You Forget?

We get up each morning to go about our day.
D'you take a moment just to pause and to pray?

As the day goes along to decide what you'll do,
Have you considered that you'll need to pray thru?

Our lives get so busy; it seems like a fraud
F'we don't take the time to consult with our God.

We get so darn busy that we seem to forget,
Not realizing, haven't talked to God yet.

He's asking us to come with our plans for the day,
But God is the one who determines the way.

So pause for a moment and settle your spirit.
Come humbly to God and He'll engineer it.

If we seek His guidance for whatever we do,
The "peace that passes" will be given to you.

Now that the day's over, got thru another day.
How many moments did you slow down to pray?

At the end of the day, as you're starting to nod,
Hope your last words weren't "Sorry, forgot you, God."

So with your eyes closing, do take time even then.
Say thank you to Him; tomorrow start again.

If God Would but Speak

If God would but speak, we often say,
Our lives would be better day by day.
We ask God to speak so we can hear.
Hopefully make His presence seem near.
With life so busy, we just don't hear
His still small voice; He's standing so near.
His words are here, right here in our hand,
Giving directions to help us stand.
Don't ignore His directions so clear;
Obedience always drives away fear.
Elijah hid in the rocks that day,
Waited to hear what the Lord would say.
Thru a powerful wind, He did not speak,
Nor when the quake shook the mountain's peak.
Then came the fire; still no voice was heard.
All prepped the way for the living Word.
Then a small voice, like a gentle breeze,
Like a whisper thru the mountain trees,
He said to the man, "You're not alone;
Please don't be fearful as you are prone.
There're many with you; I've helped them stand,
Scattered throughout this ungodly land."
God speaks just as clear to us today,
Promises strength to get thru each day.
Don't be so doubtful, but instead rejoice;
He makes it easy to hear His voice.
If we take time in quietness still,
We'll hear the words that speak of His will.
So if you find your hearing impaired,
Go to the mount; it can be repaired.

Put distractions aside, still your heart;
After some time the hearing will start.
Don't be impatient; might not be fast.
Stay till it happens, then it can last.
The more you listen, the more you'll hear;
The more you'll know His presence is near.
When God speaks softly, seldom real loud,
We learn to hear His voice in the crowd.
Knowing to turn to the left or right;
We will walk by faith and not by sight.
The faith that pleases Father above,
Faith, the witness of our grateful love.
It all starts by taking time alone—
Humbly, quietly, approach the throne.

Prayer—How Long Has It Been

How long has it been since you've been on your face,
And stayed till the answer came?

How long has it been since you've been on your face,
Sought naught but His holy name?

How long has it been since you've been on your face
In the darkness of the night?

How long has it been since you've been on your face
And persevered thru the fight?

How long has it been since you've been on your face,
Clothed in armor fit for war?

How long has it been since you've been on your face
And not thought it was a chore?

How long has it been since you've been on your face,
Bathed in His glorious love?

How long has it been since you've been on your face,
Felt approval from above?

How long has it been since you've been on your face
And sought just the Father's will?

How long has it been since you've been on your face,
Got strength, His will to fulfill?

How long has it been since you've been on your face
And set your wish list aside?

How long has it been since you've been on your face,
Only to wait and abide?

How long has it been?

Prayer—What's Our Focus

We ask the Lord to bless our day,
to make things work in every way.
Too oft our thoughts: "what pleases me,"
According to the way we see.
We've made our plans and said our prayers
And then consult the God Who Cares.
Stop! Hit rewind and start anew,
Then ask the Lord, "What pleases You?"
Then let's set all our plans aside
And try real hard to just abide.
"Where would You have me go today?"
"What are the words You'd have me say?"
And then with all the questions done,
Take time to listen to the Son.
The hardest thing for us to do—
to stop and wait to hear from You.
Sometimes the answers come real fast;
Some, we think, too much time has passed.
Whene'er they come, they're from your hand,
Lord, help us do as You command.
Then as we serve from day to day,
We'll learn to know the words you say.
Divine appointments every day
Help us to trust and then obey.
A simple cup? You're sure that's all?
'Twas hoping for an order tall;
'Twas looking for that special task.
Lord, help us do whate'er You ask.
The day will come, we'll see the Son
And hope to hear the words "Well done."

Prayer

A righteous man praying availeth much.
He seeks for the world the Master's touch.
Prays for the soul that's going to hell,
Asking for changes that all would be well.
He prays for the world as it goes its own way,
That eyes would be opened and God rule the day.
That His kingdom come and His will would be done,
In hopes that each life will submit to the Son.
That honor and glory would come to the Lord,
When lives are surrendered and Jesus be Lord.
For the will of the Lord, the righteous man prays
And defers to God's will for all of his days.
Willing to set all of self-will aside,
The surrendered life in God's will abides.
Jesus has taught us the right way to pray,
"Thy will be done." For there's no other way.

Wait, Don't Move

As life goes through its process, there'll be some changes that take place.
We know they're bound to happen, know that time will not erase.
But even in life's process, there will be lessons there to learn,
But earthly eyes oft forget the spirit also gets a turn.
We're not just made of flesh and blood; we're all a spirit too.
The influence of our spirit determines what the flesh will do.
In every situation, lessons by both flesh and Spirit.
Unless we find quiet time, our flesh just won't let us hear it.
Stories told of kings of old, sought God's guidance on their knees,
Helped them through the strongest tests, gave His word with victory's keys.
But when those kings forgot to ask when the country was at rest,
Went their own way, forsook the Lord, then sorely failed the test.
Don't look at circumstances to figure out what is best,
Or counsel friends for wisdom when it seems they've passed the test.
Our response oft determined by what's happened in the past,
Please consider this suggestion before the die is cast.
Ere you weigh the pros and cons, so you make the wisest choice,
Simply ask God for wisdom, then don't move till you hear His voice.
He's promised to give wisdom, if we'd but take the time to ask.
The response will come to fulfill His purpose in each task.
David says, "Trust in the Lord, don't depend on what you know,
In all things acknowledge Him, He'll show you which way to go."
So take some time; seek His face before you start your journey out.
His guidance is always true, so right or left? There'll be no doubt.

Wants and Needs

His promises are faithful,
said, He will make a way.
Plans known to only Him;
   it might not be today.

When we get so impatient
and want our answers now,
we just want our wants met;
   don't care about the how.

I say, "Want our wants met."
God alone knows our needs.
He's promised to provide them—
   not our wants, just our needs.

His Word says He'll give us
not a stone for some bread.
But it's He who determines
   if it's a stone or bread.

In our way of thinking,
we're asking for some bread,
but God's infinite wisdom
says, "That's a stone instead."

So again it's God's mercy
when He seems to tell us no.
Know it's for our protection
   He deems to answer so.

So what might be a blessing
   in someone else's hand
could be a great big problem
   if placed within our hand.

So when we're asking Father,
forget not—it's His will
that must be considered
as His will He fulfills.

Since we can see so little
and He can see it all,
we must trust Him for our needs
as He provides them all.

What God Can Give

Why all the emphasis on what God can give,
when all that He's done still allows us to live?
The example of Jesus speaks very loud;
His concern was just for the face in the crowd.
'Cause Jesus's thoughts were never focused on "Me";
All his focus instead was "Dad set them free."
By shedding His blood, God's wrath was set aside;
He's made the provision so we can abide.
He provided a way for us to be free,
be free from the things that can trap you and me.
Why is it we focus on what God can give,
when we should be asking, "Lord, what can I give?"
We get so wrapped up in "What's in it for me?"
We forget saying thanks for being set free.
When we're giving thanks, why can't that be enough,
and spend much less time on the "asking for stuff?"
God gives us the promise, "our needs He will meet,"
the roof o'er our head and the shoes on our feet.
The list of God's promises, easy to find;
the list, all inclusive, can just blow your mind.
Seeking the promises can get in the way
of us serving our Savior, day after day.
Don't forget your "First Love" and chase after things
the loving of "First"—oh, what joy that will bring.

Surrender

A Cross Has No Ladder

Instructions for each to "take up your cross."
To be effective, self must suffer loss.
We must be willing to set self aside,
Embrace that "death" if we want to abide.
It's hard enough to get up on the cross,
A fight to decide—"Is it worth the cost?"
The choice then to "die" is really quite bold,
But then the truth of it later takes hold.
Our "life" of the cross is hard to sustain,
Our flesh always wants to get down again.
My friend, be sure it's the cross that you choose;
There's no turning back, no ladders to use.
Crosses don't come with a ladder, my friend.
We'll be nailed there till all your days end.
Again, choose wisely to answer the call,
Then take up your cross and give Him your all.
The cross and its work we are asked to embrace,
Struggles the same for the whole human race.
Self's first inclination—just to survive—
Will do all it can to just stay alive.
Jesus has taught us we daily must die;
His teachings say more than "Give it a try."
Once you've decided and hands on the plow,
To be fit to serve, can't look back now.
There are three things about a man crucified,
But no resurrection till he has died.
If we only die once, best get it right;
To answer that test, does my self still fight.
The first thing about a man on his cross,
Can't look back now, so consider the cost.

Second, the man only looks straight ahead;
Can't see behind, so there's nothing to dread.
Third is the fact all his plans have been made.
No need to worry; the price has been paid.
We're bought with a price, no longer our own.
We stay to fulfill the Love that's been shown.
Temptation to run will be very real;
Remember, in death, life has no appeal.
We're not of this world; we serve a new King.
"Well done, my child"—the reward it will bring.

Guilty but Redeemed

"Guilty" was the verdict, not by jury but by God—
A common condemnation on all who walk this sod.
It's not unique to anyone; we're guilty of that curse
Passed down from those before us. Prone to sin, we can't reverse.
The flaw is in our DNA; it cannot be replaced
Until the image of the Lord is transferred in its place.
But till that transfer has been made, the judgment still remains,
The penalty the same for all—death—and all that it contains.
That penalty must be carried out—no process for appeal,
Unless there's a redeemer who wants to break the deal.
In God's providential plan, a redeemer did agree,
Agreed to do what must be done, redeeming you and me.
The requirement of redemption Jesus agreed to meet,
The cross, the grave, and one more thing before the plan's complete.
The death that was the penalty became the final foe.
In the res'rection of the Christ, His awesome power did show.
That act of propitiation, God's wrath be set aside,
Expressed love and forgiveness, now invited to abide.
God's plan is now completed as planned from the very start;
The goal from the beginning was for us to yield our heart.
The yielding, like a death in kind, we've each a cross to bear;
Then we thru res'rrected lives show the world that God does care.

Sowing and Reaping

We run away from danger, and we run away from pain.
Often fail to run away from the sin we should disdain.

We fail to see the danger of our failure to obey.
The guidance God has given, as we live from day to day.

The Word's for our protection and has warnings intertwined,
Telling us how to avoid having problems down the line.

There will be times of hardship that we all will have to face,
That cannot be avoided as we run the earthen race.

But why we choose to ignore the warnings God has shown,
And even tells us in His Word we will reap just what we've sown.

Grace will cover all our sins, but grace might not take away
The results of the choices where we walked in our own way.

There might not be deliverance from results of choices made.
Can but hope to be released from the price that must be paid.

Whether we're released or not, still God's grace will see us thru.
Pain could have been avoided if to the Word we'd been true.

Remember, friend, God warns us, "My children, please don't walk away,
Ignoring all the guidelines that I've given you this day.

"My ways are always perfect; they're meant to help you walk,
To live a life victorious, so it's more than just some talk."

My Way, the Right Way?

Sometimes facing a problem, I spend time in prayer,
Knowing full well that I can find answers there.
Sometimes I rely on what's been in the past,
Expecting this time to be just like the last.
There are certain instances that might be true,
but more often than not each instance is new.
What the Lord has supplied is good for today;
tomorrow might bring only rot and decay.
If I don't seek the Lord and search out His will,
then my will takes over, and His will is nil.
Because of my nature to go my own way,
I oft fail to inquire, "Lord, what should I say?"
I'm sure my solution is always the best
and seldom consider, "It's only a test."
The test is to see what my response will be;
when others around me don't seem to agree.
I turn disagreements to personal attacks,
and then my response is usually fight back.
Then the love that should always be on display,
requested by God, just does not rule the day.
If my way's the utmost for things to get done,
then know for sure, that's not the way of the Son.
If I get stiff necked and demand my own way,
I'm not being open to what God would say.
Of course, it's a given in matters of sin;
There's no room for discussion which side will win.
I'm asked to be willing to set all aside,
to walk in surrender and in His will abide.
Not even once did Jesus demand His way.
His Father's will Jesus would always obey.

What makes me so different that I get a choice
of whether or not I will obey His voice.
There just isn't room for two wills in my life.
I must serve just one or be troubled by strife.
A man double minded will be tossed about
until he surrenders; he'll struggle, no doubt.
If I want peace, I must surrender my will.
Embracing the cross will then His will fulfill.

Making Plans

When I get upset with things as they happen,
I find that I'm much too important to me.
I've programmed my mind to what makes me happy;
The end of the story, I'm failing to see.
I make all my plans and think they should happen
Exactly the way I propose them to be.
Lord, help me remember it's okay to plan,
But you determine what my future will be.
I need to be able to flex with my plans,
Remembering that you know just what's best for me.
We ask of the Lord, assuming the answer
Will come all wrapped up like we want it to be.
Remember God's will is much more important,
Because Jesus alone the future can see.
That which we ask for, we're sure they'd be blessings,
But God in His foresight knows trouble they'd be.
By His grace and mercy, He always answers;
Sometimes it's just not what we want it to be.
Remember, my friend, that God's will is perfect.
Lord, may thy will be done in heaven and me.

Making Decisions

As we walk thru life, situations arise.
Some answers not clear and questions arise.
If wise, we seek counsel of friends who might know.
To help make decisions on which way to go.
Too often we trust feelings at our first response,
And then tunnel vision can tend to ensconce.
And then just like Moses, "It happened before."
It'll happen again; don't ask anymore.
Sometimes worldly wisdom seems to apply,
But it's often at odds with the Spirit's reply.
Ofttimes we'll study and books we will read;
We search to find wisdom of how God will lead.
Then there are times when we'll seek God in prayer.
We know boundless wisdom will always be there.
Often read Scripture to look for a guide,
And there can find answers to help us decide.
Brother James said it well in one short quote:
"We should humbly accept all words that they wrote.
The words as they're written have pow'r to save."
Not only from sins, but the desires that we crave.
Sometimes we don't like the answers we find.
So we go back to prayer—will God change His mind?
We fast and we pray, "God please help me find
A way to justify what I had in mind."
Self puts on blinders, then our focus is set.
Not often content till that focus is met.
Oh, that our attitude would constantly be,
If God's words are written, enough that should be.
There's covering, of course, f'we heed God's word,
When we follow hard, every word that is heard.

Follow God's council to the nth detail,
We'll ne'er have to pray that seeds planted would fail.
Obedience is always a test of two wills.
Trust and surrender says which will gets fulfilled.
That struggle continues this side of the grave;
The balance is tipping—which one will you crave?

Jars of Clay

Just vessels of clay, we're right from the wheel.
We're made by His hand, however He feels.

The vessels are made of water and clay,
Smoothing rough edges, for use every day.

Only the Potter knows from the start;
The task for each one He holds in His heart.

No two are alike, never quite the same,
So pleased with His work, calls each one by name.

Why such great care does He take with each one?
Always rejoicing as each one is done.

Some jars are fancy and some very plain,
Some jars for wine and some to catch rain.

Whatever the task for which you're designed,
Yield to the Potter, in service resigned.

Don't look at the jar and judge the outside.
Look at the treasure that's hidden inside.

Light's the true value in each single jar—
The presence of Christ illumines each jar.

Needing each other to get the job done,
We're showing the world the life of the Son.

Each jar is needed and equal in worth,
Serving the Potter, throughout the whole earth.

Instead, Think of Others

We look at the world 'round us and look for release,
To be removed from it all, that we'd be at peace.
We have looked for deliverance, and no, that's not bad,
But if that's our only focus for sure "we've" been had.
If your goal is to be cloistered safe in our ark,
Tell me, how can we help those who live in the dark?
Are we not called in Scripture to be salt and light,
To help those in living darkness to walk by sight?
How can we share the truth that helps set people free,
If our concern is safety for "mine and for me"?
If we're afraid of the world that's in such a mess,
We don't understand Christ's great commission, I guess.
Sends us out to the wolves, even though we're like sheep,
To prove to the world those He saves He can keep.
Sure, the world is a mess, and the end could be near,
But we won't be much help if we're hiding in fear.
Their future is at risk, and they've got to be told
Before it's too late and all things start to unfold.
So let's scrap all our plans of constructing our ark,
And with the light of the truth shine forth in the dark.
Share the truth of the gospel, "that Christ came to save."
By this expression of love, miss eternity's grave.

I Will versus Thy Will

I will—thy will the war thru the ages.
I will—thy will the battle still rages.

"I will" is selfish with much to defend.
"Thy will" is loving, will give to the end.

"I will" is lonely, where one stands alone.
"Thy will" is loving, where none stands alone.

"I will" brings chaos, heartache, trouble, and strife.
"Thy will" contentment while walking thru life.

"I will" is shallow and serves only one.
"Thy will" is gracious and serves everyone.

"I will" is sin at its most basic form.
"Thy will" is foreign to man's basic norm.

"I will," unholy, will cause me to stumble.
"Thy will" is gracious and helps me be humble.

"I will" is ungodly and seeks for a high.
"Thy will" is fulfilling; His presence is nigh.

satan said, "I will," and caused nothing but strife.
Jesus said, "Thy will," and gives us new life.

"I will" has no place in God's perfect world.
"Thy will," will help us be free from this world.

We can say "I will" and walk all alone.
Or say "Thy will" and ascend to the throne.

Seasoned Response

Seasoned by grace, our responses should be
a life like the Savior others can see.

A soft-spoken word usually turns away ire,
but harsh-spoken words will sure light a fire.

Still we blame the tongue for all that goes "south";
instead it's the heart that speaks through the mouth.

Blaming the tongue, we can ignore the heart,
the place where all change is needed to start.

David was right when he said, "Here's the start."
"Oh, God, please create in me a pure heart."

Help me clear my heart of all that's myself,
so I won't react when threats come toward self.

Dead like the Savior, we're instructed to be,
to all of the things so important to "me."

Buried in Christ, unaffected within,
by the trappings of self, the basis of sin.

To be free to respond, seasoned by grace,
we can show the world a glimpse of His face.

Servant or Slave

Each of us is born a slave, and a slave, that's all we'll be.
The key to life is bound up in "whose servant will we be."

From birth we are slaves to sin, plagued by patterns from the fall.
Adam chose to eat the fruit, and that caused us all to fall.

All sin starts with falling short of the standards God has set.
Choose the way "I" wants to go, then rebellion's course is set.

Let's go back an age or two, before man roamed the earth.
Some angels up in heaven had a problem with their worth.

One angel took the forefront and then boldly spoke his mind.
satan said, "I'll be like God; all creation will be mine."

With those words he spoke that day, a new way of life began.
The world of "I will" started and became the curse of man.

Before that even happened, a plan had been set in place,
a plan for Christ the Savior to redeem the human race.

The plan was set in motion for a new world to begin.
Jesus named that world "thy will," and it sets us free from sin.

To choose the world of "I will," "I'll be free," don't be deceived;
the bondage will be greater, exalting self—you'll be deceived.

To choose the world of "thy will" begins a different life,
one of love and gratitude and a servant's way of life.

In servanthood, the choice to serve is the greater way of life.
According to the Master, bringing peace and never strife.

The choice is set before us, to which world will we be slave;
the choice is ours to ponder: "Be a servant or a slave."

In servanthood find freedom, like your heart is yearning for,
a life of full surrender, as we serve the risen Lord.

The Beginning

Who needs a Savior? Who says that I'm lost?
Almighty God did, so consider the cost.
Ere we can be saved, we must know we're lost,
needing a Savior no matter the cost.
Perfection is required if you want in.
That means you can fail with one little sin.
Here's a quick story to set records straight;
a real understanding will open the gate.
Before the beginning, God had a plan.
His goal and desire—to fellowship with man.
It all started out with only one law,
don't eat of the fruit—miss the fatal flaw.
We couldn't do it; we went our own way.
We ate of the fruit and spoiled the whole day.
It looked like God's plan had been dealt a blow;
sin caused a break in the fellowship flow.
A short time later, He gave more commands;
a clear complete list of all His demands.
Complete compliance was needed, said He,
if you want heaven and be there with me.
The law's intention—to show us our need;
bring to the light and expose our misdeeds.
Misdeeds divide us from Almighty God;
even best efforts can't us get to God.
In spite of all that, it's not over yet.
God has a way for His price to be met.
Sacrificed blood must be innocent and pure.
The life of the Christ displayed that for sure.
Blood that was required for freedom to pay.
Jesus met the price on the cross that day.

His expression of love, beyond compare,
a model for us with others to share,
speaks of a Savior for others to see,
explains how "That Life" can set people free.
Free from the bondage of life to the law,
free to serve others—a much higher law.
God's grace, a free gift—there's no way to pay.
Jesus is the Savior; it's God's only way.
It's been written down, chiseled in stone;
Jesus is the way to approach the throne.
Accept Christ's sacrifice made on the cross,
have eternal life without suff'ring loss.
Denying yourself and live for the Lord,
eternal life and heaven's your reward.

Work of Art

The Master completed a true work of art,
unique in its own special way.
In all of creation, there's only one you,
each of us in our own unique way.

Fearfully, wonderfully woven together
to bring glory to God each day.
That only happens in total surrender
as our all on the altar we lay.

Although there's a process before the paint dries,
'twas finished on conception day.
I say it is finished, 'cause God sees the end,
yet the process goes on each day.

The paint will be drying; the clay won't be set
until we face our final day.
Each classic, you see, a project in process
with changes made day after day.

Though not completed, each moment is perfect
when it is done the Master's way.
Don't be so impatient, learning contentment,
and give God control of your day.

When we can say "Amen, Lord, let it be so,"
we're giving up having "my way."
That's the way of the cross that God calls us to
and walk in His way every day.

Why Are There Tests?

Dear Lord, please help us understand
our life's completely in your hand.
There's not a trial that we walk thru
that's not been preordained by you.
You have a goal thru every test;
for each of us you know what's best.
Your plans to prosper all our days
help us rejoice in all your ways.
We think prosper—life of ease,
So we can do just as we please.
You think prosper to mean live right,
to give us strength to fight the fight.
Sometimes when tests are very tough,
the test is, will we trust enough?
Enough to say, "Thy will be done."
In full surrender to the Son.
Sometimes when tests are very hard,
we're sure that you've been caught off guard.
That you'd allow a test like this,
you did in fact your promise miss.
You didn't protect us as you should;
too quick forget, you're only good.
You never said a life of ease
you'd give to us if we'd say please.
You said your grace would take us thru
if we would put our trust in you.
You also said, "In all rejoice."
To make the point it is by choice.
In choosing thanks, our will resigns,
and proves to others I am thine.

Be thine to serve in all you ask,
to willingly embrace each task.
Acknowledging that you are King,
Give up controlling everything.

Who Needs to Change?

Let the Word of God speak, and I will listen.
If I don't agree, who needs to change?

If I listen hard and my heart feels uneasy,
if I don't agree, who needs to change?

It's all been written down; the guidelines are true.
If I don't agree, who needs to change?

God's ways—unchangeable, they just remain true.
If I don't agree, who needs to change?

Now the question becomes a matter of wills,
not based on feelings—who needs to change?

It all boils down to an issue of trust.
If I have issues, who needs to change?

Confessions are simple, but changing is not.
Lord, I have been wrong; I need to change.

Surrender's not easy; I don't want to die
to my own feelings. Lord, help me change.

We will finally be changed on that glorious day,
but until that time—Lord, help me change.

Walk in the Light

This earthly tent will one day fail, and time will be no more.
Eternity will then unfold upon a "distant shore."

There's one great choice we have to make, determines where we'll be;
It will be either light or dark throughout eternity.

Just to be more specific, the choices we have to make:
Will Jesus be the Lord of all, or we'll our own way make?

The choice that each of us must make revolves around our will,
The selfsame struggle Jesus fought, obeying Father's will.

"I am the Light," Jesus has said. The choice is up to you.
Your future will be determined by what you choose to do.

Too often we reject the Light that's there for all to see,
And walk in pure rebellion and do what pleases me.

We hate the Light because our sin we do not want to see,
And hopefully we can avoid accountability.

We show how we hate the Light by running from the Light
And walk in utter darkness, not conscious of our plight.

"I Am the Way, he Truth, the Life; the choice is up to you.
With Light to walk the narrow road, to guide what you should do.

"It is my will that none should walk upon that darkened road,
But rather walking in the Light will ease your heavy load.

"It's full surrender that I seek, eternity to gain,
and with your will set aside, you'll hear that sweet refrain.

"Refrains the angels cannot sing; it's only the redeemed
Who sing the song salvation brings, much sweeter that it seemed."

The Spirit Within

One question that rises again and again:
The fruit of the Spirit—when does it begin?
Is it a progressive, a gradual process?
Or is it completed when we first confess?
But that's not the question I want to address.
But "How much of the Spirit do we possess?"
As the Spirit moves in, "Is the move complete?"
Or is there a need that the transfer repeat?
Are we teased by only receiving a part,
A mischievous game to discourage our heart?
Unable to act the way we know we should,
'Cause the power's not there as we heard it would?
I'll challenge that thinking—please consider this:
We're not shortchanged the Spirit's power remiss.
We're told that the Spirit's a firm guarantee;
That all God has promised us will come to be.
When the Spirit moves in, just one bag is used.
That's all that He needs—one bag; don't be confused.
When He moves in, He leaves nothing behind
that we have to search for and hopefully find.
It's not the Spirit's lack that we think we see.
The real problem is, there's way too much of me.

The Shepherd's Test

When we're resting on His promise
and trying to abide,
there's no room for stress and worry.
It's peaceful by His side.

We find within the shepherd's psalm
a very simple test.
Just adding words of "when" or "if"
will answer every test.

If the Lord is truly Shepherd,
then what have we to fear?
When the Lord is truly Shepherd,
our life will be so dear.

So if we're stressed or worrying
and in a troubled mess,
then we're not trusting in His love
to see us through each test.

Stress does not come from Father's hand
but from our own reply.
Peace comes from trusting in the Lord.
He is our soul's supply.

"Cast all our cares," you've heard it said,
and He will give us rest.
We don't have to worry at all.
He really knows what's best.

The Sermon on the Mount

When Jesus taught the lesson there on the mountainside,
He gave to us the challenge, "Do you want to abide?"

To me it is a struggle; my thoughts are not the same.
I need to change my thinking, to be called by His name.

It's upside down and backward, so seems this Christian life.
The tenets we're to deal with cause flesh much grief and strife.

Turn the other cheek, we're told, give more than what they ask;
Be kind to those who hurt you, to bless is quite a task.

Do not curse your enemies; give love to those who hate.
And when you're treated poorly, never retaliate.

It's best not to get angry; anger can lead to hate,
And that's the same as murder. Forgive, don't hesitate.

If I would be forgiven, then I, too, must forgive,
To show the world the diff'rence and like the Savior live.

All these thoughts seem upside down that Christ has asked of me.
Found the one that's upside down, it isn't Him—it's me.

The struggle set before us, that self takes quite a loss,
'Tis nothing to consider if hanging on my cross.

If self is still defensive when challenged with this loss,
Then I can know for certain, I've not embraced the cross.

Called to take our cross and die and lay all self aside,
In love serve one another; Christ can then be glorified.

The Law

The law came not to save us all;
it can never set us free.
The law instead has shown us
just how lost a soul can be.

That which brings us to the knowledge
of the problem of our sins
can never set a sinner free
and absolve us all from sin.

We see the standard of the law,
realizing it can't be reached.
Someone has to bridge the gap
if heaven's to be reached.

And that we each need a Savior;
one to pay the price for sin.
Willingly gave up His life
so that we can now begin.

To begin to walk in freedom,
free to fellowship with Christ.
The fellowship of suffering
and res'rections power with Christ.

He gave up His life so freely
to fulfill the Father's plan.
The sacrifice was needed
to redeem lost, sinful man.

The righteous robes we need to wear
come not from the things we do.
Rather, they are Christ's alone—
His gift to me and you.

It's His grace that justifies us,
not by works of any law.
Grace comes as a loving gift;
blood required by the law.

Yet the only way we can walk
in surrender to the Lord,
each of us pick up his cross,
then walk Calvary with the Lord.

The Gate

How long will you halt?
How long will you wait?
How long will you stand
with your hand on the gate?

What is it that holds you
and makes you stand still?
What is it that keeps you
from doing His will?

What does the world offer?
What does the world hold,
that keeps you from breaking
away from its mold?

The gate that's before you
leads straight to the cross.
To a time in your life
to consider the cost.

To pass thru the gate,
you will have to choose.
With one path you win;
choose the other, you'll lose.

The one path is wide
and appears to be level,
filled with nice things
but is built by the devil.

The other is narrow
and looks to be hard,
is filled with rewards
'cause it's built by the Lord.

Brothers, don't tarry;
sisters, don't wait.
No longer stand
with your hand on the gate.

Choose you this day
whom you will serve!

The Bucket List

We've all heard the phrase called "my bucket list"—
The list of all the things we'd like to do.
Then the race becomes to check each one off,
To do it all before our life is through.

Paul had a list of a similar sort,
But 'twas rather "to be" than things to do.
Then suggested that we follow his lead,
The list be the same for me and for you.

He shared his list with the Phillipi folks
In a letter to friends he knew so well.
Shared his first, foremost, and utmost desire
Along with the story he loved to tell.

To know the Christ of the resurrection,
And to know the power that was displayed.
To have fellowship in His suffering
And the opportunity that is made.

To get to wear his robe of righteousness,
To receive the prize which He set aside.
Then to be a citizen of heaven,
In a glorious body we will reside.

Then Paul concludes, "Now that's my bucket list.
Won't you please alter yours to be the same?
Because by doing so, you will stand firm,
Then all you are brings glory to His name."

Pride

Why?

This came as a result of my sister's home going. My nephew, David, called me to share a dream that he had about being in heaven and seeing his mom. Her back was turned toward him, but he knew it was her. Jesus was standing between them, and every time David tried to look past Jesus to see his mom, Jesus moved to block his view. In desperation he cried out, "Why? Why?" Then Jesus shared the thoughts of this poem. As we learn to trust the Lord more, the times of why will become fewer and farther apart. Why can be asked in a proper way, to get understanding, but when we totally trust in the Lord's faithfulness, the need for understanding will be obliterated.

"Why did this happen?" We'd all like answers now
so we can understand all the when, where, and how.
It's our bent to control everything that we see
that makes us ask why, because my focus is me.
The Lord asks to trust him in all that He does;
there will be times His answer will be "Just because."
Let "because" be enough, a sufficient reply;
when the timing is right, you will understand why.
"For now there's no chance you could ever comprehend,
because you just can't see your way through to the end.
But till then please trust me. 'Twill be for your good;
There will come the day when all will be understood."

The Struggle of "I"

Why do we struggle—still contemplate "I"?
When Jesus says, "Take up your cross and die."
If we would follow, then our self must go;
Nailed to the cross—full surrender will show.
The difference with us and the way Jesus died,
we must die daily so we can abide.
The life tried to save we surely will lose,
If we choose to lose this life He can use.
Paul says it different but much the same thing.
"All your self-will to the grave you must bring
To be resurrected, live a new life."
Serving Him only will never bring strife.
The only time strife will enter the fray
Is when we attempt to have our own way.
If we've died to sin, no longer a slave,
Then service to Christ is what we will crave.
Our struggle with sin, signif'cantly less,
When our life's goal is Jesus to bless.

The Root of It All

When God gave the list of His ten "don't dos,"
It gave us a choice—now we have to choose.
We think that the list is rated by score,
The first is the worst; it's much worse than four.
So on and so on, we rate one thru ten,
Avoiding the first again and again.
The last on the list deals with our desires.
We're not to covet, 'twill light many fires.
The fire of desire, "what we feel we need";
Be careful, my friend, in truth it is greed.
Since covet's the last that's seen on the list,
It oft gets ignored; we often resist.
We think since it's last, consider it least.
But really, my friend, it acts just like yeast.
It doesn't take much to spoil the whole mix;
If not dealt with quickly, we're in a fix.
Let's take a moment to give it some thought,
Then can address it the way that we ought.
The first four listed are twixt God and me,
But then five thru ten, between me and thee.
Let's define "covet" as having my way.
Whate'er the subject, it will spoil the day.
In all of the nine that come before ten,
"Covet's" the problem again and again.
"I'll" choose what "I" wants; I will not face loss
And totally ignore the work of the cross.
In our call by Christ to willingly die,
Must take up my cross; there's no room for "I."
The first sin recorded, "I" will have my way;
I will be like God and rule every day.
When I'm the focus and exalt my name,
It's just no diff'rent than was satan's claim.

Micah 6:8

The command given in Micah 6:8
gives us a different way of living.
The focus that's seen, like that of the Lord,
is a life that's focused on giving.

Instead of us asking what we do for Him,
He asks us to focus on others.
The request that's made is really quite simple:
practice fairness and kindness toward others.

It seems so simple when read on the page,
but put into practice—a whole different game.
To walk in His steps, our lives have to change;
our lives must be sacrificed in His name.

The sacrifice spoken of—dying to self,
that self-will has always died slowly.
Self always struggles; it just won't give up
on the plan of not being more lowly.

Only in dying is life truly found,
dying to self we are no longer bound.
Bound by the struggle to set ourselves free,
free from the struggle that keeps egos bound.

It's Not about Me

The more I learn of the Master,
The more I can clearly see
That living life for the Master,
'Tis true, "It's not about me."

If I want to be like Jesus
In ways that the world will see,
Then I have to live for others.
'Tis true, "It's not about me."

Try as I might to be holy
And do everything that I can;
I can overlook the real truth.
'Tis true, "It's not about me."

Jesus has set the example.
He set His self-will aside
To serve the Father and others,
To prove "It's not about me."

He asks us to serve each other
Looking to each other's needs.
Then He will be our provider
And prove, "It's not about me."

Isaiah told us the story
What happens to those who serve.
He provides without limit
To prove "It's not about me."

Hanging on the Old Rugged Cross
Looking down thru all the years,
He saw that it was worth it.
And proved "It's not about me."

Grumble and Argue?

"Grumble and argue" speaks of me in control,
Not being willing to surrender my soul.
Won't surrender the right to choose my own way,
To make my own choices to live day to day.
The example we set for a world that's lost
Will only appear as we embrace the cross.
The children of God should be blameless and clean;
Don't grumble or argue; your light will be seen.
Above reproach in a world that's gone bad,
It will happen as we rejoice and are glad.
It's God who is working within and without,
To bring His own will and good purpose about.
So how can we grumble and argue with God,
With the thankful heart of the children of God?
When God is the author of all that we see,
Our heart should trust God, not depending on "me."

Mine

Before I could crawl
and before I could walk,
actually even before I could talk,
the most oft-spoken word and focus of action
was centered around this simple reaction:
"It's mine, and I want it;
it's mine; you can't have it."
From morning to dawn,
it became quite a habit.
The name of the habit for all of mankind
is selfish, self-centered—it's basically "mine."
Why do we hold on and fight day to day?
It's because we want to have our own way.
Then Jesus steps in and seeks our devotion
and asks us to change one simple notion.
He asks, "Can you trust me to meet all your needs?"
He asks to try this one simple deed:
"It's others I want you to worry about,
to help them along without any doubt.
As you look to others to carry their load,
I'll be your light as you walk down life's road.
You really can trust me; I haven't failed yet.
I'll help you break the mold that's hard set.
The mold that is set by the nature of man
will all melt away in the palm of my hand.
I want you to serve your fellow man,
setting self aside as a part of the plan.
The rest of it's easy; it's already done—
life everlasting with Father, Spirit, and Son."

Pride—The Problem

Pride got satan in hot water first.
Isaiah tells us he just said, "I will,"
and started the spiral that takes us downhill.

"I'll be like God and do as I please.
No one can tell me what I cannot do;
I have decided that I am equal to you."

God says, "My children, please, listen to Me.
Don't be rebellious and go your own way.
Choose Me to follow to live day by day.

"My rules and suggestions don't benefit Me.
Yes, they are rules, yet more like suggestions,
'Cause you can choose your own course of action.

"My will is that no one would ever be lost.
As My word has said, 'There's only one way
to walk close to Me in victory each day.'"

So to bear the image of Christ in your life,
Must pick up your cross and walk the same way.
You will find that your joy lasts day after day.

Finishing the Race

A Home Going

The death of God's servants
Is such a sweet smell.
He brings them all home,
That all may be well.

We think it so sad
When they're called away,
Not thinking the Lord
Has shown the best way.

The righteous are taken,
And no one takes thought.
It's called deliverance,
That now they are not.

Deliverance from problems
Potential or real,
God's love and mercy—
Now that's a big deal.

When death calls us home,
No time for goodbyes,
We'll find our rest in
The sweet by-and-by.

A Servant's Life

"A Servant's Life" is for my mom when she passed away. When Grandma died, Mom inherited her rug loom, and she used it until the day she sold her house and moved into an assisted living home. Mom made and sold all types of rugs—anything from a mug rug for a coffee cup to pet dish mats to area rugs. She even made a rug runner that now rests in a museum in the town where she was born. She was constantly at her loom weaving or helping someone. In this poem, the word WOVEN is capitalized in honor of a lady who gave herself to others, myself and my sister included, and also helped raise four of her nieces and nephews after their mom passed away. All in all, she was a very special lady. I know, as she walked through the gates of heaven, she heard, "Well done, good and faithful servant!"

Her service is over. Her life's work is done.
The only thing left is rejoice with the Son!

She faithfully served Him in each little task,
Cheerfully doing whatever He'd ask.

She never sought glory or from this world fame.
Her only life goal: "serve in Jesus's name."

The tasks seemed so little—thought no one would care.
In service to God, still, her life He would share.

On this side of glory, Mom never did know
The gift of service—how much it would show.

The words, "If you love me, you'll keep my commands,"
Were not taken lightly in this servant's hands.

You see, each little task that she did in Christ's name
Was WOVEN together, and it honored that name.

Those who willingly serve with a thankful heart
Have a special place in the Father's heart.

Then Mom's life was changed in the blink of an eye.
The Lord called her home—no time for goodbye.

Mom's service is over; her life's work is done.
The only thing left—rejoice with the Son!

Death Redefined

Why do we default with a fear of death,
Finding dread in the thought of our last breath?
Why does death first lead to negative thought,
Instead of thinking the way that we ought?
The Scriptures teach us our hope is secure,
Of what waits ahead 'twill always be sure.
They also promise a firm guarantee,
That all God has promised will come to be.
Hebrews says, "Live like you're just passing through;
A better home has been promised to you."
Many before us looked straight ahead;
By faith they passed on with nothing to dread.
The faith commended of those in the past,
Knew the troubles of this life would not last.
Instead looking forward, chose to believe,
The promise of God, they'd someday receive.
Their eyes weren't focused on their "day to day";
Instead their "new country" drew them away.
If they'd been looking at what they had now,
they could be drawn back—lose grip on the plow.
Willingly faced death by various means,
Because the promise through faith they had seen.
Willingly traded the now for the when;
With no fear of death, they'd do it again.
The world was not worthy that they remain;
"Look forward with hope" was their only refrain.
To borrow some thoughts of a poet of yore,
("Death Is Not Death" by Charles Kingsley 1883)
Death redefined, now diff'rent than before.
We struggle with death; we think it's the end,
The fact is, it's really life's true start, my friend.

When this life is o'er—a blink is too slow;
We'll be with Jesus, if you didn't know.
Death is not death for those who believe;
Christ is the answer, the pardon receive.
Death is not death when it ends doubts and fears.
Death is not death when it dries all our tears.
Death is not death when our healing's complete.
Death is not death when we sit at his feet.
Death is not death when mortality flees.
Lord, help us choose immortality please.
Death is not death at our homeward call.
Death is not death; there is no death at all.
Death is not death; Christ has gone before.
Death is not death; there's no sting any more.
Death was defeated that day at the tomb.
Death's empty grave now a cold dusty room.
For those who believe at "Death's final call"
Will find themselves in that great banquet hall.

Departed Friend

Fare thee well for now, my friend. This day's been bittersweet.
You're no longer here with us; you sit at Jesus's feet.

It's for sure that we'll be sad to see a good friend go.
But oh the joy that we know that's on your face will glow.

We don't understand it all, just why your struggles came.
But yet we know those struggles brought glory to His name.

Your faithfulness to praise Him in spite of such a trial
Has left a glorious witness; of that there's no denial.

Faith that lasted thru your test gives us a world of hope,
That Jesus keeps His promise: "I'll give the strength to cope."

He said He'd never leave us, and your life proved that out.
You gave us an example that we just cannot doubt.

He gave another promise, that He'd provide a way
To give us strength and comfort, to help us thru our "day."

Your "day" lasted many years, but some think way too short.
Yet it lasted just as long as Jesus's first report.

The "days" numbered in His book, that He had set aside,
Were faithfully completed; He's called you to His side.

If we were really honest, we'd know we must rejoice,
Knowing you've received your crown, lived faithfully by choice.

As I said, "for now my friend," there soon will come the day;
We will be reunited on that great wedding day.

Eternity together worshipping at His feet—
My friend, what could be better, and what could be more sweet?

You just went on before us and showed to us the way.
Well done, good and faithful friend. We send you on your way.

What Would You Do?

We're oft asked this question: Just what would you do
If your last numbered days were made known to you?
First let me remind you that God knows that day.
It was planned before your life got underway.
Would you feel panic and filled with regret?
Troubled by concerns you hadn't met yet?
Or would there be joy, the race almost o'er?
The joy of knowing that you'll wander no more?
Would we stop and ponder and then start a list,
And then try to make sure that nothing gets missed?
The first on the list is confession for sure;
Betwixt God and me, have my actions been pure?
Have I confessed all the wrongs I have done?
Did I repent? Don't want to miss even one.
Of course there's our loved ones we know we will miss.
Got to make sure they get that one final kiss.
Might think of relations where things were not right,
Often regret—that was the silliest fight.
Then remember thoughts of our fellow man
Whom we had mistreated—corrections we'll plan.
And then there's the sorrows of love not expressed,
We might feel guilty over what we've repressed.
We might list some sorrows of things that we chose.
"If that hadn't happened, then heavens, who knows?"
Now please let's consider the question that's asked:
What would you do before all those days passed?
That question, my friend, though asked with all cost,
Should just be directed toward those who are lost.
If we've walked with Christ, for sure each day's a test,
Most of those problems should have been put to rest.

The exception toward loved ones, the only that's true,
There can be the day they'll again be with you.
This statement is hard; get your toes out the way.
Let me take this question a whole different way.
When that day is known, why should behaviors change?
If "in Christ," that thinking should really be strange.
Now since we're in Christ, let's look at the list.
Most of those reactions should never exist.
If we'd be more faithful to live as Christ asked,
Our last few days would not be such a task.
The list to correct the wrongs we had done
Would then, my friend, be a much shorter one.
Less time would be spent in time's sad grip;
More time looking forward to the upcoming trip.
Paul says in Ephesians that sunset's too late
To make things right, using just two words: "Don't wait."
Take care of it now, ere the sun can go down.
You'll never wake up, start the day with a frown.
In his letter to Tim, Paul says it real clear,
What our response should be as that day draws near.
I've done what was asked, I have finished the race;
I've labored real hard to end up in first place.
There's now been a crown that's been laid up for me,
To give back to Jesus when His face I see.
If the "Royal Law's" kept in all that I do,
It's called success when I love God and love you.
If that is my goal for each day that I'm given,
I'll have fewer regrets as I'm ushered toward heaven.
Paul says it again: our goal should always be
To bring glory to Christ so that others will see.
If we'd live life as righteous, there'd be no shame,
Just honor and glory to His holy name.

Where Did Mother Go?

"Where Did Mother Go?" is dedicated to Cilla's mom, who passed away in 1984. We went home after Anna's memorial service, and the Lord gave the words for the following poem. Over the years we have been able to send it to many others when their moms passed away. She was an amazing lady.

"Where did Mother go?" you say.
You think she's really gone.
Just look inside you, and you will see
she's been there all along.
Each day that she was with us
is memories stored away
and kept in hidden places
and saved just for today.
Tho' Mother's body's gone from us,
she still lives in our hearts.
We're looking forward to the day
we never more will part.
'Twill be so happy on that day
to see her face to face,
but after that, our joy will be
to look on Jesus's face.
Altho' you might be sad today,
Mom's really filled with joy
to be before the Lord she loved—
more than a child with a toy.
Christ the Lord has called her home
to be there by His side,
to worship, praise, and honor Him
and ever more abide.

The End

When life begins to fade away,
when all our strength is gone,
looking to His righteousness
will help us carry on.

We fight against remembering
the way things used to be,
forgetting how much change we'll face
as our time begins to flee.

Our lives are just but a vapor
according to God's plan.
We think we're indestructible,
but that's our prideful man.

We lose our strength, maybe our sight,
and other problems come.
Don't dabble with discouragement
'cause not all is lost, just some.

Remembering "This too shall pass,"
and that day will arrive,
We will exchange this mortal flesh
for one that really is alive.

Graduation Celebration

On August 21, 2006, my sister Nancy passed away, three years after Mom went home to be with the Lord. In planning for her memorial service, with me being the last family member, I knew I would have to share something. While trying to put some thoughts together, I stopped for a moment and thought about the positives on her side of the ledger: She's with her Lord and Savior, no more pain or the sickness she had dealt with for so many years, she was with our mom and dad, and she'd finished her race. As the list grew, the thoughts of sorrow were replaced by thoughts of gratitude and rejoicing. The thought that came to mind was "What do I have to be upset about?" My thoughts changed to "It's time to celebrate." But I have to admit to a little bit of envy mixed in, because she had finished her race and was now at total peace. Those feelings became so strong that, for me, the day of Nancy's memorial service was more like a party than a time of sorrow. It was such a joyful occasion for me that by the end of the day, my face hurt because I had been smiling so much. Scripture tells us that there is a time to grieve. We all grieve differently, but Scripture reminds us in I Thessalonians 4:13 that those who believe in Christ grieve with hope. With the hope in knowing that there will be a day when our hope will no longer be needed, because our hope will become a reality. As all these thoughts were rolling around in my head, the Lord gave me the words for this poem, reminding us that it's time to celebrate. Again, Scripture tells us that the Lord has all our days written in His book, and the day of our "graduation" or "home going" is already known by Him. Also that promise that what the Lord has planned will come to pass. Nancy's life has been completed, and I'm sure she's celebrating.

Our days are all numbered; the Lord knows each one.
They were all written down before they'd begun.
From living to dying it's such a short trip,
Yet we hold on real tight, won't loosen our grip.
We hold on really hard to things that we know.
When we fear the unknown, it's hard to let go.
It should not be unknown, God's Word's very clear,
When this flesh gets removed, then Jesus we're near.
If we choose to believe everything God's said,
When we're facing our death, what is it we dread?
Of course there's our loved ones we don't want to leave,
But we'll see them again, if they, too, believe.

A part of the problem, we've not learned to die;
We're told to die daily but don't want to try.
If we'd put into practice this one little test,
If it's focused on me, then my soul's not at rest.
'F we learn to die daily, then heaven's in sight.
Our thoughts will be Godward; we'll do more things right.
It's also a struggle to let someone go;
For sure we will miss them, and our grief will show.
Let's stop for a moment and think this thing thru,
What God's word has told us—do we know it's true?
If we walk with Jesus, then death has no sting;
Our journey's completed, with joy heaven rings.
The gates are wide open; a saint has come home.
Forever in glory, they'll never more roam.
Would we be so selfish, just to ease our pain,
To hope they could somehow come back once again?
We should be rejoicing that they've been set free.
Of all the hindrances that bind you and me,
We should be rejoicing—they sit at His feet.
They've finished the battle; God's plan is complete.
We should be rejoicing; they have no more pain.
"It's well with my soul" is now their refrain.
We should be rejoicing; all sickness is gone.
Their hopes been realized, that new day has dawned.
Their robes are washed spotless; there are no more stains.
No longer encumbered with mortal remains.
We talk about heaven, look for Christ's return,
Too often our thought is, so we will not burn.
There's much more to heaven than just an escape.
Forever with Jesus, all sorrow's erased.
All the joys here on earth will fail to compare
When all heaven's splendor with Jesus we share.
The splendor we look for, it's not streets of gold;
It's just Jesus himself—the truth has been told.
The things of this world will grow strangely dim.
As our hope's realized, we are now with Him.
There'll be no more darkness, for Christ is the light.
We'll worship the one who makes everything right.

Grandpa Brotherton

Cecil, the dad of a family of eight kids, was known as "Grandpa" to many. I think he considered everyone he knew as family. Cecil needed bypass surgery and went in for the surgery and came out fine. After a short period of time, things made a turn for the worse. He had to go back to the hospital, and they had to open him again. They found his chest was full of infection. Cecil slipped into a comma on November 28, 1984, and did not regain consciousness this side of his eternity. On May 14, 1985, the Lord called Cecil home. I believe it was Christmas of '84 that the event of this poem took place. All the family and many of us "adopted" ones were at his bedside to worship, pray, and praise the Lord. Cecil, still in a comma raised his hands with tears on his cheeks. The week before Cecil's memorial service, the Lord started dropping these thoughts as I was literally driving down the freeway between jobs writing down the thoughts as they came. What a blessing it was to be a part of such a special event and to be able to share these thoughts with the family.

With friends and family gathered round
To worship and to praise,
And when he couldn't say a word,
He lifted his hands in praise.
And through that simple, faithful act
His spirit's voice was heard,
Letting those around him know,
"It's time to meet my Lord."
A tear would trickle from his eye,
Mixed with sorrow and with joy,
The sorrow of the parting
But the joy of going home.
Cecil's walk is over now,
With joy he ran his race,
And now he has the promise,
For he looks on Jesus's face.
Thank you, Lord, for your great love
That called our brother home
And brought to end the suffering—
His final step toward home.

We know that there will be a day
When we will meet again
And stand together side by side
To praise your glorious name.
So till that day we meet again,
With love we say farewell.
Thank you, Lord, for the love you gave
Through Cecil Brotherton.

Thanksgiving

Thanksgiving

A heart of thanksgiving, this season will be
the focus of many, their blessings to see.

'Tis more than a season for us to think of
the ways to be thankful for gifts from above.

Thanksgiving's a lifestyle directed by faith,
trusting in the Savior, who controls our fate.

When we can say thank you for what comes our way,
we've surrendered the right to control our day.

Surrender is trusting "He" knows what's best,
our character building each time there's a test.

The plans He's established for only one goal:
to bring us to glory; He's ransomed our soul.

When finding you're tempted to gripe and complain,
then always remember this simple refrain.

With joy and thanksgiving let's come to the throne;
give glory and honor that's due Him alone.

Then—

Follow this exercise; it'll help you, no doubt.
Count all of your blessings; list every one out.

Then when you're tempted to grump and be sad,
you will have the reasons to rejoice and be glad.

Set Free from Me

We will never know this side of the grave
to our sin nature, how much we're a slave.

We know what we want but don't always do,
then there are times when we don't know what we do.

Try as we might, just as hard as we can,
perfection is not a part of the plan.

Perfection's not needed to win the prize;
thru Jesus's blood we're clean in God's eyes.

In spite of our failures time and again,
we're still forgiven; there is no again.

Once we've been forgiven, score's never kept;
we're free from the bondage o'er which we've wept.

With sins forgiven and so far away,
like east is from west, there is no replay.

So always be thankful; give thanks with glee,
knowing that we have been set free from "me."

Rejoicing—Faith's Response

As we follow Christ, rejoicing's a must,
For the Scriptures state, it shows whom we trust.
Trusting's an expression of faith, that we know,
When we're rejoicing our trust level will show.
Rejoicing's more frequent through faith as it grows;
That expression to all, a trusting heart shows.
Our rejoicing will bubble from deep within,
Knowing God's in control ere trials begin.
God's promise given—'twill all be for your good;
Someday, the final outcome will be understood.
Through Christ we've been promised a bold guarantee;
The Spirit's our promise all will come to be.
The Spirit's influence to work all things out,
For God's will and pleasure to bring it about.
Is rejoicing easy, or is it a fight?
What is our first response when things aren't just right?
If rejoicing is hard when things don't seem right,
Are we trusting by faith or walking by sight?
For us, is God's faithfulness more than an act?
In our daily life, is it fiction or fact?
If I can't rejoice until after the fact,
The question arises: "Is my faith intact?"
We can get discouraged if desires aren't met,
But please don't forget—God's not finished yet.
We're urged to look forward, beyond what we see.
Hold fast to the promise what God said will be.
We can't know the outcome that faith will produce,
But rest assured, 'twill be for His Kingdom's use.
If we behave rightly, rejoice in faith's hope,
Others might question us: "How is it you cope?"

So when tempted to seek relief from life's stuff,
The response you might hear, "My grace is enough."
Paul and Silas rejoiced and the way was paved;
They both stayed imprisoned, but people got saved.

If Only This, If Only That

If only this, if only that, we all too often say,
And do not concentrate enough on what we have today.

"If only" speaks of malcontent and also "wanting change."
We wish that our circumstances would somehow rearrange.

If only this, if only that, contentment cannot say.
Instead a thankful contrite says thanks for every day.

Thanks for what you've given me says, "I'll let you be God,"
And that I recognize your hand; my life's been planned by God.

If I could learn to trust you, Lord, right from the very start,
Every time a test came up, I'd bless you from my heart.

Because as I learn to trust you and believe your written Word,
I find that you have promised me those blessings in your Word.

You'll only give what we can stand with joy in any trial,
And as we see your hand provide, no problem with denial.

Please help me, Lord, to be content with what you've given me.
So I can always be rejoicing—in the "Hand That Feedeth Me."

Greener Grass

Grass always seems greener
When seen from far away.
We can only see the tops,
But below it looks like hay.

The reason "grass seems greener"
We choose not to be content.
Looking for a brand-new thrill,
Our self-will, will not relent.

Be thankful for provisions
From God's almighty hand.
And always be believing
That God has all things planned.

The secret's to be happy,
Which will help your heart stay pure.
By giving thanks in all things
And be in God's love secure.

If we should choose to grumble,
With what seems to be our lot.
Then who are we upset with?
It's with Him who knows the plot.

We want to blame each other
And deny the cold hard fact.
If we would but be honest,
Anger at God, it's a fact.

Brother, look around you,
Seeing blessings from God's hand.
Thankful hearts will never gripe;
They accept what God has planned.

His plans will always prosper
Even though sometimes they hurt.
Remember, they're only temporal,
And they will not always hurt.

A thankful heart allows us
To see with the eyes of faith.
We will see the harder times
As the building blocks of faith.

Count Your Blessings

A Poem for Sis

No wonder we're discouraged or even depressed;
We don't count our blessings and how we've been blessed.

When our mind quickly returns to what has gone wrong,
The focus on cares will rob joy from your song.

"The Song of Salvation" no angel can sing;
Counting your blessings will His presence bring.

With all our focus on cares, we will tend to doubt,
Forgetting God said, "I'll work all things out."

We're told to place all of our cares in His hand;
When he carries the load, it's then we can stand.

The list of promises, all found in the Book,
Are forever before us—take time to look.

Our doubts come from forgetting the promises made;
The first to remember—"The price has been paid."

If we keep that in focus, all else seems to pale
When compared with God's love, which never will fail.

When we're tempted to grumble o'er worries and fears,
Start counting your blessings and dry all your tears.

Then the tears of confusion will dry on your cheek;
When counting your blessings and His mercies seek.

When we stop and say, "Thank you," for each little gift,
We're resigned to His Lordship and our spirits will lift.

Sometimes counting our blessings can be quite a chore;
If we're focused on problems, we need to trust more.

But when faced with a struggle and heart filled with grief,
When we utter, "Thank you," it will bring us relief.

So remember, God's faithful, give thanks to the Lord;
A joyful existence will be your reward.

Choosing Thankful

Lord, help me be thankful for what comes my way,
and help me be thankful for each brand-new day.
Your glorious mercies are new every morn,
to lead me and guide me and walk thru life's storms.

Your mercies so tender can cause me to rest,
even in the midst of a turbulent test.
They're more than just helpful to walk thru a trial;
your mercies surround me, should be no denial.

Choosing to be thankful makes statements of trust.
To walk in God's mercies, then trusting's a must.
By trusting, we're saying, "God, you know the way,
to lead me and guide me each step of each day."

In trust we acknowledge that God's in control;
When deciding what's best, God has the lead role.
He knows the beginning, can see to the end,
and knowing full well, where eternity we'll spend.

He wants us to choose, "just to trust and obey,"
in the words of the song, "there's no other way."
Then we learn to trust Him and give up our will,
Exactly like He did, on His way to the hill.

When we take up our cross and do as He asks,
He then gives us the strength to do any task.
He will never ask more than what we can bear,
will provide us a way; there'll be no despair.

God tells us, "Be thankful" in all that we do,
that blessing so boundless will come back to you.
The blessings that come back, not just for pleasure,
instead to know God's peace—that is our treasure.

Here's just a reminder of where we should start.
"Let's give glory to God, with a thankful heart."
Then I'll say it again, just so we don't miss:
"A loving, thankful heart brings nothing but bliss."

Our Glass

We look at our life as compared to a glass.
"Half full or half empty?" the question we ask.
We look at the level to judge the supply,
half full or half empty, we shape our reply.
When the level is low, we think that it's bad.
We think we're short changed; it makes us feel sad.
When the levels are high, things seem to be right,
then we tend to relax and not be uptight.
It's in God's economy, how the glass gets filled;
the level reflects just what God has willed.
The issue is not "the level of fill."
The level's determined by God's perfect will.
Our needs we've been promised, oft more but not less;
the secret's contentment, relieves all the stress.
Contentment and thankfulness—they're both the same thing;
they both will acknowledge that the Lord is King.
God gives the level in our "glass of life."
With thankful contentment, we will know less strife.
When all's said and done and we look at the glass,
it's not the level; it's the size of "our glass."

Rejoice

"Time and again, I've told you rejoice.
I'll say it again: it's time to rejoice."

Is there a time when rejoicing is wrong?
Or is there always some room for a song?

A song of thanks comes from a rejoicing heart.
A song would sure be a good place to start.

Always rejoicing—a statement of trust,
trusting in Jesus—it's always a must.

Rejoicing and trust are never apart,
they both will be found in a thankful heart.

A safeguard for you—I'll tell you rejoice.
A rejoicing heart is always a choice.

A thankful heart, too, is always a choice.
Even in sorrow, there's room to rejoice.

A trusting heart is responding to love—
Love boldly stated by the Father above.

Rejoicing, thankful, and trusting—all three
found in the heart of a person who's free.

A person who's free of worry and strife,
rejoicing in Jesus and living new life.

Rejoicing and trust say, "I am content,"
feelings from which I won't have to repent.

Christmas

Jesus, Prince of Peace

That first Christmas Eve, when peace was foretold,
Angels proclaiming a message so bold.
Could Israel know peace, with Rome such a pest?
Heartache and trouble, just no chance to rest.
Goodwill unto men—He gave of His best.
Peace unto all on whom His favor rests.
We hear the word "peace"; they heard "Shalom."
That which they'd yearned for would finally come home.
Finally! Peace! Now Rome would be on its way.
With those tyrants gone, peace could rule the day.
A savior was coming, they could believe.
Their longing for peace, they would finally receive.
What they had in mind was a hard-handed king
Who'd set justice right, then peace he would bring.
Now back to the angels—few people heard.
"The event to bring peace has finally occurred!"
The shepherds went looking. Could it be real?
The "King" who would save them, 'twas a big deal.
The prophets foretold a "Savior" who'd rule;
Born in a stable? Take me for a fool?
How could he change things? What good could he do?
Could he bring peace, make the prophecies true?
Here's where they went wrong: they just couldn't wait.
The Prince of Peace with them, some filled with hate.
Now down thru the years, man's goal's been the same.
Our cry of "Peace, Peace"—the name of the game.
It seems so futile, as much as we teach.
It's always elusive. It's just out of reach.
The peace usually sought first—peace in the land.
The peace angels spoke of, can't touch with your hand.

The peace that was offered—peace of the heart;
Trusting the Savior is where you must start.
Believe that all things are touched by His hand.
Working together—the good He has planned.
The peace we're offered, though, comes at a cost.
Complete surrender, self-will becomes lost.
The favor they spoke of, and peace that we seek—
Both will be given to those who are meek.
It's not just by works that His favor is known.
By the surrender of self it is shown.
Don't be discouraged or filled with despair;
The peace that you seek will one day be there.

The Present

The present was wrapped ere time began.
A gift prepared for the heart of man.
'Twas all wrapped up in the pages of old.
The prophets spoke of a plan so bold.
This present contained the perfect plan.
The plan to redeem lost, sinful man.
Lost, for sin had entered the garden,
Where sin had caused man's heart to harden.
Set in motion before Adam fell,
the plan prepared to make all things well.
To soften again the hearts of stone,
God packaged grace, man's sin to atone.
This gift was different from all the rest.
The Father knew when the time was best.
The plan first revealed on Christmas day.
When God sent His Son to show the way.
Thru years of silence the plan took form.
Obedience was His daily norm.
Thirty years later the time drew near
To reveal the plan and make it clear.
In three years, He showed what it would take.
Relations restored for the Father's sake.
The Father knew man needed a lift;
Now was the time to unwrap the gift.
In the garden the paper got torn,
completely unwrapped on Sunday morn.
The paper and bows completely gone.
The gift was revealed just before dawn.
Jesus came forth; now death has no sting.
The whole creation started to sing.
Songs of victory, the battle's been won.
Songs of praises to honor the Son.

Songs of worship, of wonder and awe.
Songs declaring we're freed from the law.
Songs of thanks stating, "Now we are free."
Songs confessing He loves you and me.
Songs of salvation, saints only sing.
Songs of reverence in awe of the King.
Thankful songs declare grace was revealed,
Condemnation has now been repealed.
The list of songs goes on without end.
Open your heart; rejoice with me, friend.
Tho the gift's opened, plan's not complete,
Till each one He's called "sits at His feet."

Christmas, Easter, and the Cross

Christmas day, when Christ was born;
Easter, resurrection morn.
Each is such a special day—
important steps along the way.
In between those special days,
the Christ, in death, atonement pays.
Finished story needs three days;
thru Jesus's death the price He pays.
Remember this; don't forget:
the Cross is most important yet.
Jesus died upon that tree
to give to us salvation free.
Jesus only, Christ alone,
the gift of God, sins to atone.
Try to add a single thing,
the Gospel dies; a death it brings.
Christ and the cross stand all alone;
price was paid, sins to atone.
His resurrection sealed the deal,
Eternal life can now be real.
If we try add a single act,
the gospel is no longer fact.
Grace alone completes God's plan,
of Him redeeming sinful man.

Christmas: The Gift of Love

The Word became flesh and joined man on earth;
Christmas set aside to honor His birth.
Angels delivered the message with joy;
Told the shepherds about the birth of a boy.
Not just any boy was born on this night,
The message delivered while they were in flight.
A message of peace to all of mankind,
The only hope that will bring peace of mind.
Then they proclaimed that the Savior had come
To save the whole world, not only some.
"You'll see the babe on a bed full of hay."
Immanuel, God is with us today.
To live His life an example to see,
To show us all how He wants us to be.
His birth was foretold by prophets of old;
Be born of a virgin, really quite bold.
That He'd descend from the line of a king—
Salvation to the whole world He would bring.
O'er hundreds of years and by many men,
The prophecies true again and again.
They all came to pass, not one left behind.
Look for yourself; it will bring peace of mind.
The facts are all there—they can't be denied.
They all came to pass, so nobody lied.
With a record like that, how can we doubt
The rest of the book? The facts are all out.
The odds of one person meeting them all—
The oddsmakers say that it's really quite small.
With that kind of acc'racy, best not deny
And say that the rest is just a big lie.

We struggle so hard with God's stated plan;
That plan brings salvation to every man.
The reason we struggle—"I can't earn my way?"
"No, it's a gift," and God has the last say.
The gift was presented on that Christmas Eve,
The best gift that man would ever receive.
The love of the Father, granted to all,
Paid the full price, now redeemed from the fall.
The fall when man chose to go his own way,
Instead of trusting that God rule the day.
It's really quite simple to receive this gift;
You must recognize your soul needs a lift.
When recognized and accepted as fact,
You will see a change in how you react.
The life that submits to God's saving plan
Reopens that gift of Love to each man.
So Christmas is not a one-time event.
When lived all year long, will help others repent.
A life filled with Love brings glory to God.
Shows serving others is not all that odd.
To wrap it all up, this gift from above,
The boldest statement, the gift of God's Love.
All of creation rejoiced at this birth;
The gift, God's Grace, had now joined man on earth.

Christmas—The Birth and the Cross

Christmas, what a special day,
when the King of Kings was born.
Born not as a king but
in a stable so forlorn.

The good news was spoken first
in the middle of the night
by a whole bunch of angels—
gave the shepherds quite a fright.

Wise men came to honor Him.
They came from far away,
for they had observed the stars,
found a king was born that day.

Christmas story's fun to tell,
but that's only telling part.
Actually, as the story's told,
It is really just the start.

The angel's words, spoke months before,
told of more than just a birth.
The Savior of all mankind
would come here to live on earth.

Come to live and then to die
for the price that must be paid.
The sacrifice for all mankind
upon Jesus Christ was laid.

To fulfill the law's demand,
a sacrifice must be made.
The spotless Lamb—crucified,
then the debt was fully paid.

Three days later—Sunday morn,
when the stone was rolled away—
Christ came forth in victory,
and death's sting was torn away.

Mary saw the circle close
as the angel said 'twould be.
The birth, the life, then the death,
then came forth for you and me.

'Twas the Night before Christmas

'Twas the night before Christmas, and the world unaware.
Their Savior was arriving; did they even care?

Though there were many looking to clean up their home,
That the scourge of their earth would go back to Rome.

Because their focus was locked on just earthly things,
Their eyes completely blinded to a "newborn" King.

To the one who would suffer, to set their lives free.
The full price of redemption one day on a tree.

But back to the first moment, the good news was told.
All the shepherds were frightened by angels so bold.

They spoke of peace to men living on the earth.
They'd find a manger in town, the place of His birth.

So they went forth to witness what they had been told.
Then they all shared the good news with joy; they were bold.

On this night before Christmas, the words just as true.
It's the same presentation, a Savior for you.

Of the peace that was spoken to shepherds of old,
You, too, can experience, just as it was told.

But the peace angels spoke of had a small test:
The peace is for men on whom His favor rests.

That peace can relieve you of all of life's strife;
By God's enabling grace, a new way of life.

A new life of surrender to Jesus the King—
When we make that decision, all heaven will ring.

Advent's Message

We celebrate Advent to remember Christ's birth;
The one day celebrated throughout the whole earth.

Advent not started till the fourth century—
In Latin, "a coming," to look forward, you see.

The four weeks preceding that day set aside,
Helps us remember the Christ came to abide.

Now, advent's not just a one focus day,
There's another one coming, the Scriptures all say.

We know Christ has come but should still look ahead;
He's coming again just like He had said.

"I will come again," He was quoted to say.
"Be ever alert, for you won't know the day.

"Keep your hearts ready, have a listening ear.
The signs of my coming will keep you from fear."

With great anticipation look toward that day;
All tears will be dried and all pain gone away.

A life of perfection, we'll be glorified,
And then with our Savior forever abide.

On that day we'll finish a marvelous race,
And then we shall see Him, at last face to face.

With crowns in our hands, to be laid at His feet,
We'll meet our Savior at God's great mercy seat.

Easter

All Alone in the Garden

With joy set before Him He went to the cross,
Without hesitation considered the cost.

He knew from His Father away He would be,
But went there to save a lost sinner like me.

Much more than the beatings and all of the pain,
Separation from Dad, much worse than the pain.

All alone in the garden, though others were there,
He begged of the Father to ease His despair.

Twice He asked of the Father "to let this cup pass,"
But knowing full well His own will He'd pass.

But the pass that he spoke of was not "to avoid,"
His word "pass" translated "to go through," not "avoid."

Now think of the Father, the pain in His heart,
Turned His back on His Son, the joy of His heart.

But with Father so holy, could not look on sin,
Turned His back on His Son, while bearing our sins.

It was God's perfect plan, a gift to us all,
Sacrifice needed to redeem from the fall.

The act of redemption—it had to be made,
Innocent shed blood on Jesus was laid.

Fulfilled what was written to make true the word,
Proved after three days dead—"I am the living Word."

The credit line's balanced; the price has been paid,
And now the atonement for us has been made.

At the right hand seated, His Father's right side
Seated, now praying, so we can abide.

We're called to be different, to be salt and light,
To show a lost world how we can live right.

Now with others in mind, we set self aside
And act like our Savior and walk by His side.

Easter '06

Nailed to the cross—satan thought he'd won.
He just didn't know the power of the Son.

Three days later, the price had been paid.
That Sunday morning, He rose from the grave.

Before He died, He said it is done.
Now eternal life through Christ has been won.

Eternal life—how long can that be?
This side of heaven, we just cannot see.

One day we'll know, when we've run the race.
Jesus will call us—we'll be face-to-face.

That glorious day will last forever.
We'll be by His side and live there forever.

No more of pain and no more of sorrow.
We'll live there "today"; there'll be no "tomorrow."

Easter '07

All night long, a trial was held. 'Twas a mockery and a sham.
Held at night in several courts, the whole thing was a scam.

Very early in the morning, Pilate said, "Let it be so."
Instead of turning Jesus loose, he said, "Let Barabbas go."

Orders given: "Beat the man." Mocked and beaten close to death,
Then walked up Calvary's Hill, with the instrument of death.

Then at noon the world went dark; course was set, the die was cast.
Without Father, all alone, three hours later, breathed His last.

"It is finished" was His cry upon that old rugged cross.
Never attempting to save Himself—loved the world, endured the cross.

With the joy set before him, pleased to do the Father's will,
He shed his blood for you and me that day on Calvary's hill.

On resurrection morning, when the stone was rolled away,
With the tomb completely empty, fear held the guards at bay.

An angel sat upon the stone, telling them, "Do not be afraid.
Seek not the living with the dead; see the place where Jesus laid."

The clothes were folded, He was gone; the body could not be found.
The guards were still there frightened, just like dead men on the ground.

The women ran to tell the men what had just been told to them.
"He is risen, He is risen!" then remembering what He'd said.

He'd talked about His dying and then coming back to life.
That death would be defeated—we would have eternal life.

Eternal life to spend with Him from now thru all the ages.
We can know, the story's told; it's written in the pages.

Easter '08

They did not know, those disciples of old
The rest of the story yet to be told.
All that they knew was their leader was gone;
They did not know that a new day would dawn.
Their hope had been He would save them from Rome.
That then they'd be free and get back their home.
Now He was dead and their dream disappeared,
So life would continue just as they'd feared.
They didn't understand what Jesus had said:
"Three days later, I'll rise from the dead."
Then came Sunday morning—oh, what a day!
Went there to mourn, found the stone rolled away.
The grave was empty; His body was gone.
Jesus had risen sometime before dawn.
He'd broken the bonds of death and the grave;
The tomb was now just an old empty cave.
On Friday, despondent, they just didn't know
That Sunday morning would bring quite a show.
Early that morning, there was quite a stir.
"He's risen, not dead." At first they weren't sure.
Early that evening, it was verified.
'Twas true, He had risen; He'd walked by their side.
They'd walked and they'd talked and even broke bread;
'Twas proof beyond doubt that He was not dead.
Now with joyful hearts, they could dance and sing.
In Jesus, they'd found the true risen King.
Risen, victorious, the battle is o'er;
We do not have to fear death any more.
Now as we look back way down thru the years,
We have our struggles and battles with fears.

Never lose sight of this one simple fact:
The world was changed by that one glorious act.
So when you find yourself laden with fears,
Remember the message passed down thru the years:

"It may be Friday, but Sunday's comin'!"

Easter '09

The supper was over; He'd just washed their feet.
And now in the garden, in prayer they would meet.
After singing a hymn, they went down the road.
He needed to pray, for He carried a load.
He knew what was coming, prepared all His life;
To walk this road that was laden with strife.
The plan set in motion before time began.
"To restore fellowship between God and man."
'Twas in that first garden, the plan was revealed.
Man disobeyed and fellowship was repealed.
That first sin had caused a division to form
Between perfect God and now-flawed human form.
The requirement by God that blood must be spilled,
To restore relationship must be fulfilled.
The symbols and shadows of blood in the past
Now found their completion in Jesus at last.
Now back to the garden, the story goes on.
It was mostly completed way before dawn.
That night in the garden, He struggled in prayer.
All His friends went to sleep, thought that they didn't care.
He asked of His Father, "Please help pass this cup.
But I know it's your will; I give my will up."
Surrender completed, was now time to go.
Officials and soldiers put on quite a show.
So bravely they came in the dark of the night,
When they all fell down, must have been quite a sight.
Then they took Him away, betrayed by a kiss.
They held trial at night, thought most people would miss.
The mockery and beatings tore His body up.
He knew in advance; it was part of "the cup."

The final conclusion the Cross on the hill.
Now two-thirds of the plan the Cross would fulfill.
"It's finished," He cried in the darkness of night.
He gave up His Spirit and ended the fight.
Later that night, all His friends, grieving with tears,
Thought it was over and trembled in their fears.
"'Twas good while it lasted; 'twas three glorious years."
Said, "I'm going fishing" and blinked away tears.
With much disappointment and hearts filled with grief,
They all walked away with their shaken belief.
Then came Sunday morning; there was quite a din.
They found the grave open; two brothers walked in.
It's true, yes, it's true. He has risen indeed.
The works now complete to redeem Adam's seed.
The victory was total, 'twas utter defeat.
The grave lost its power—no chance to repeat.
He said it was finished and meant what He said.
With satan defeated, we've nothing to dread
Though satan will buffet and try to destroy,
The Cross was victorious, defeating his ploy.
If in all that you do, you submit and resist,
satan will flee! Of your life peace will consist.
The pattern's established for victory within,
Surrender self-will, have less trouble with sin.
So live as forgiven and walk in the light.
By serving each other, the Savior's in sight.

Easter 2010

From the beginning of time, the prophecies read,
His heel would be bruised, but He'd crush its head.
Then at just the right time, as the crushing drew near,
With the battle lines drawn, Christ had no fear.
Thru agony so bitter and the pain He did bide;
It still was His choice, the cross where He died.
All of hell was rejoicing—thinking they had won;
They'd finally defeated God's precious Son.
Other prophecies spoke that the vict'ry'd be won.
But now it looked like they'd all come undone.
But God's plan still in motion, satan just a pawn;
This step was completed just before dawn.
How could this be victory? Death seems so complete.
Once you're dead, there's no chance to repeat.
But wait just a minute, the story's part told.
Come Sunday morning, the stone had been rolled.
An angel sat guarding there just inside the door,
Grave clothes folded—"Not here anymore.
No longer be seeking Him here with the dead,
You see, He has risen, just like He said."
Those prophecies completed, but yet there are more
That speak of the victory we can't ignore.
Jesus will come back, and every knee will be bent
In honor—submit to the life that was spent.
A life spent to rescue all those who believe,
And now thru Jesus, their pardon receive.
It's over, it's finished, and not just for some.
The story's completed—His Kingdom has come.

Easter 2011

As He came down the hill off the Jericho road,
His heart was heavy, for He carried a load.
He stopped on the road near the top of the hill,
Wept as He pondered what He'd come to fulfill.
"I wanted to comfort and hold you so near,"
As He reached for His cheek and wiped off a tear.
Then He rode into town with throngs all around,
With fronds from the palm and their cloaks on the ground.
While their shouts of "Hosanna" were filling the air,
The Pharisees grumbled, were filled with despair.
"Blessed is the King who is coming today."
The Pharisees cried, "Stop it; don't talk that way,"
Told Jesus to hush the hysterical crowd.
"If I do, then these rocks will cry out real loud."
Now that was Palm Sunday, the end drawing near.
He kept moving forward without any fear.
He cleansed the temple and taught more lessons too.
As His time drew near, knew just what He must do.
Resolute in His actions, His jaw was set.
Was fully aware the goals that must be met.
In spite of this knowledge, His joy still held fast.
His Father's will would be completed at last.
His will to restore fellowship with mankind
Before Eden's garden had been on His mind.
The plan of the ages was almost complete;
The price to restore Jesus knew He would meet.
With the Father's pleasure, the Son with His joy,
satan didn't know his part was a ploy.
Now back to the story that's yet to be told:
Events yet to happen, as prophets foretold.

Now's time for Passover, mem'ries of the past.
How God had delivered His children at last.
First time, shared in haste, they were ready to run.
The process for exodus had just begun.
The Angel of Death passed them over that night,
By the blood on the door, if they did it right.
Many years passed since they first shared that meal.
First time, types and shadows, this time it was real.
But this meal was diff'rent; 'twas not shared in haste.
After they'd finished, wrapped a towel round His waist.
His example of service is not just desired;
If we want to follow, then it is required.
Next scene, the garden, agonizing prayer.
He prayed all alone, though others were there.
The agony so bitter, He sweat drops of blood.
The weight of it all came on like a flood.
His cry to the Father to "let this cup pass"—
Not a plea to avoid but through it to pass.
'Twas the plan before time, the way it should be,
The cost of redemption for you and for me.
His will to surrender to do Father's will,
He knew that to "pass" meant His death on the hill.
The joy set before him was more than enough,
to help Him embrace this assignment so tough.
The soldiers arrived, took Him captive that night,
Betrayed by a friend, with a kiss by torchlight.
A trial with no justice, from beginning to end.
In the midst of it all, denied by a friend.
Passed between courts, back and forth like a ball,
Two diff'rent verdicts at each judgment hall.
In the court of the Temple, all cried, "He must die."
"But I find no fault" was Pilate's reply.
The verdict was rendered; the mob got its way.
"Must be crucified." Then they led Him away.

They mocked Him and beat Him, could not recognize.
Thru the blood and the thorns, still the love in His eyes.
Half dead from the beatings, they led Him away.
They hoped He'd be dead by the end of the day.
Beaten and bloodied, then nailed to the tree.
He said, "I am thirsty." They said, "Let him be."
The sky then grew dark as clouds covered the sun;
The final throes of His death had now begun.
"Father," He cried, "Why have you gone away?"
Had to walk it alone, 'twas no other way.
The end now was near, a struggle each breath.
In a few moments, it would end in His death.
"Father, I trust you, it is finished," He cried.
Gave up His Spirit, bowed His head, and then died.
A quake shook the earth, then the curtain was rent.
From top to bottom, that's how the tear went.
The Holy of Holies now open to all;
The very first time since the garden, the fall—
The fall when man sinned—he did not obey.
Adam ate of the fruit, chose his own way.
Now back to the story, thought death was the end?
That's only half of the story, my friend.
The prophecies spoke of three days in the grave.
Sunday morning it became just an old cave.
"Messiah, He's risen!" His body was gone!
That final foe beaten some time before dawn.
He's risen victorious, at Father's right side,
To make intercession, for us to abide.
To wear the name Christian, then we must die too.
Surrender in death will bring freedom to you.
To preserve myself, I must deny the cross;
Res'rection power comes when life is a loss.

The Savior's Love

The love of the Savior, we can't comprehend.
The garden, the struggle, sweat, drops of blood,
Anguish and agony came on like a flood.

He asked of the Father, "Please let this cup pass."
Three times went alone to pray this same prayer,
Each time returned, found friends sleeping there.

The plan set in motion; they knew where He'd be.
The priests and the guards with lantern and spear—
In the darkness of night, no people to fear.

The trial was a mock'ry, a hoax and a sham.
Passed back and forth with no justice at all,
The Lamb to be slaughtered, said nothing at all.

Ridiculed and beaten, a crown made of thorns,
Flesh torn and shredded, could not recognize,
But yet thru it all, still the love in His eyes.

Last night before supper, He said to His friends,
"I've eagerly waited to share this meal
Before I must suffer." 'Twas part of the deal.

With the joy set before Him, endured the whole thing.
For love of the Father, He went to the cross,
Spent His life's blood, so we wouldn't suffer loss.

He already knew the whole series of events.
From the start to the final outcome and all,
The plan was made before man took the fall.

In total surrender, He embraced the cross.
Endured the beatings and all of the pain,
Knew if it was needed, He'd do it again.

Now then, it's Friday, some time before noon.
The trial's now over, His friends at a loss,
Completely despondent, Christ nailed to the cross.

Then total surprise as the day became night.
He dealt with two thieves, one on each side,
Then cried, "It is finished," and gave up and died.

But once was enough—yes, the price had been paid.
The curtain was torn from the top to the floor,
Holy of Holies, not banned any more.

The love of the Savior, we can't comprehend.
Now seated in heaven at the Father's right side,
Throws His arms open wide. "Please come and abide."

The Cross and Some Nails

The standard's so high,
I know I can't do it.
No matter what effort, I'll fail.

And try as I might,
the efforts are wasted.
No matter what effort, I'll fail.

Earn my salvation
and make it to heaven.
No matter what effort, I'll fail.

Salvation is free.
It's a free gift of love.
The price was a cross and some nails.

Jesus was willing,
the price of redemption.
The price was a cross and some nails.

Now eternal life
is ours for the taking
because of a cross and some nails.

So now it's our turn
to be an example
and embrace the cross and the nails.

So lay down our life
in bold imitation,
embracing the cross and the nails.

Bold imitation
of Jesus on Calvary,
embracing the cross and the nails.

Will speak to a world
that is lost and dying,
of Jesus, the cross, and the nails.

There's no greater love
than to lay down our life,
embracing the cross and the nails.

Living that life brings
encouragement to them,
to embrace the cross and some nails.

Garden of Love

He loved the garden, often been there before.
Favorite place to get away.
He'd meet Father there, together in prayer.
Learn plans for another day.

This night was different. With a heavy heart,
He really went all alone.
Though others were there just to join Him in prayer,
Them sleeping—He's left alone.

He cried out in pain, sweating great drops of blood,
And asked for the cup to pass.
But not to avoid—He knew He came to die,
Knowing the cup would thus pass.

It wasn't the death that He came to fear.
The cup, He knew He would drain.
His most hated thought—of being away
From Father—gave Him great pain.

The cross He could bear without much despair;
He knew 'twas His Father's will.
With joy He'd endure the pain of the cross
That day on Calvary's hill.

In spite of the dread, and all of the pain,
He went to the cross alone.
He died there for us so we could be free,
Making a way to the throne.

The grave could not win, could not hold its prey;
The plan was finally complete.
He rose from the dead, now at God's side,
Waiting at the mercy seat.

The Promise Confirmed

The sun refused to shine that noon; the afternoon grew dark.
The events that were taking place were sure to leave their mark.
Drawn to approach this gruesome scene, my knees became so weak.
But could not stop approaching, for the truth I had to seek.
Hanging on rugged crosses against the darkened sky,
I saw a silhouette of three men, all condemned to die.
The attention, though, was focused on one out of the three,
Hung there on the center cross, for His life he made no plea.
Instead the plea He clearly uttered: "Father, please forgive!
I place my life into your hands so in turn that they might live."
Why was it He had to suffer so—to meet that brutal cost?
The law required that blood be shed so to redeem the lost.
Events continued to unfold; one thing became so clear:
He'd been so badly beaten that the end I hoped was near.
Then with a shout so loud and clear, there was no sense of doubt;
'Twas not a cry of despair, but a glorious victory shout!
"It is finished" was His cry, then hung His head and breathed His last.
The veil torn top to floor confirmed that promise of the past—
The promise that there'd be the day of relationship restored,
Purchased by the precious blood of Jesus Christ the Lord.
Now that it was over, the crowd began to drift away.
I couldn't leave, my shoes like lead; compelled, I had to stay.
Pondering the day's events, with my heart still asking, "Why?"
I could not wrap my head around why Jesus had to die.
Then all at once I realized that I'd been unaware
That it was His love's response, for my sins had nailed Him there.
Actu'ly, now the truth is known; He didn't die just for me,
But for every soul who'll ever live throughout eternity.
As He was dying on the cross, He looked ahead in time,
And on the list of names He knew, my friend, were yours and mine.

The Plan, Completed

With Jesus's pronouncement, the process began.
The process to redeem each lost, sinful man.
A condition from which nobody can hide;
since our nature's corrupted, we just can't abide.
The presence of sin and a just Holy God
will never exist on the same patch of sod.
From the very beginning, God had a plan,
desired to walk and have fellowship with man.
Fellowship was broken when sin had its way.
The plan for redemption shed blood had to pay.
To have communion with God reinstated,
a perfect, clean life must be demonstrated.
Since we can't do that, an alternate plan
God had enacted to fellowship with man.
With our robes so wretched, polluted by sin,
the presence of God, we just can't get in.
We can't clean the stains of sin started by Adam;
we can wear clean robes of God's second Adam.
Robes cleaned by perfection to us were imputed
when by the shed blood our sins were commuted.
To stand before the throne with God face-to-face,
we must wear the robes that Christ's act did efface.
His righteousness, ours—it's a legal decree.
Our sins were commuted that day on the tree.
All the requirements were met on that day;
for the shedding of blood, sin's price had to pay.
Free from the mastery of sin in our life,
so we can now walk in the newness of life.
The door is now open for us to abide.
In total freedom, we can walk by His side.

The Party's Over

The party finally started when Judas, the priests he went to see;
When he agreed to thirty pieces, demons shouted out with glee.
Glad to see those first steps, thought it the beginning of the end.
Rejoicing grew still louder with His betrayal by a friend.
Then in the garden, nighttime arrest added joy all around.
Exuberant, started dancing. While led away, He was bound.
Overjoyed with lies told that night in the courtyard of the priest,
They'd prompted those who spread those tales from the greatest to the least.
Condemned then in a Roman court, 'twas much to their delight,
The end of their vict'ry party was for sure within their sight.
A small glitch brought a shiver; Pilot said, "No fault I find."
"I now wash my hands," he stated, mostly just to ease his mind.
The final verdict rendered found Him guilty, condemned to die,
Found favor with the crowd that night, in one voice yelled, "Crucify."
The mocking, beating, torture, and pain, now thought that they could win;
All control and destruction of mankind would finally begin.
Led up the hill, outside of town, as the prophets had foretold.
They forgot what the next chapter said, in red letters, real bold.
All the demons cheered and snickered as they nailed Him to the cross;
Blinded by pride were unaware that His death would mean their loss.
They grinned with satisfaction. Death's process was underway.
With Jesus dead, his influence gone, chaos would rule the day.
Then came a sound that stopped them short. Their attention turned about.
"It's finished!" Not a surrendered end, but a glor'ous victory shout.
In agony they realized they'd been duped, used as a pawn
To start the final process. 'Twould be revealed ere Sunday's dawn.
Now in total disarray, all their joy completely done,
They'd lost! God was victor'ous—the resurrection of the Son.

The Lord's Supper

I've eagerly awaited this meal we would share,
Depicted to show you just how much I care.
Tonight, a remembrance of what's gone before,
The night that they brushed blood over the door.
But from this night forward, it won't be the same.
This last sacrifice—guaranteed by My name.
This sacrifice needed, the price must be met,
'Cause what's gone before hasn't paid the full debt.
It's just been a shadow of how things must be.
Tonight, no more shadows; the debt's paid by me.
The plan is completed—God's wrath set aside,
No more be considered by those who abide.
This bread I am breaking will help you recall
My broken body that I'll lay down for all.
This cup, too, a symbol, but this time it's new;
My blood will be shed as redemption for you.
The table's been set, all are welcome to dine;
The required sacrifice is totally mine.
Come to the table; there's no more sacrifice.
There's naught you can do to add to the price.
To be considered, my friend, give it serious thought.
To think of this supper the way that you ought,
Don't take it lightly or as commonplace;
The value's too high, My expression of grace.
Be sure to examine the shape your heart's in;
With simple confession, be cleansed of your sin.
If you know of an ought with those in your life,
To come to the table, get rid of that strife.
With that taken care of, as pure as can be,
Partake of this table in remembrance of Me.

As you stop to consider to partake or not,
Make this thought foremost in your heart as you ought.
Don't forget it's by grace that this invite's for you.
It's about what I've done; it's not what you do.
Your sins can't be stronger; don't run away.
Forgiveness is given, for grace rules the day.
Your sins are buried in the depths of the sea,
Far as east from the west, not remembered by me.
The old celebration was "What's yet to come?"
The new party's better. Won't you please come?
This meal should be taken with joy, can't you see,
As oft as you do in remembrance of Me.

The Last Supper

So many times, they'd shared this meal,
but this would be their last.
He said, "I will not eat again,
until this kingdom's passed.
I'm going to be gone a while.
But then, when I return,
we'll all share a banquet table
with those whose hearts I've turned."
The meals that they had shared before—
remembrance of the past.
The night death's angel passed them by;
from Egypt they were cast.
The blood brushed on the doorpost
passed over those within.
The symbol of the perfect lamb,
to set us free from sin.
The feat of the deliverance
from Pharaoh's evil grip—
the symbol of our soul set free
for one eternal trip.
The Last Supper would be different,
the Word would be fulfilled.
The types and shadows of that past
in Jesus Christ were filled.
The perfect Lamb was sacrificed.
The price was paid in full.
Jesus's statement: "It is finished."
We're blood washed white as wool.
On Sunday morning came the dawn.
Salvation's plan was done.
The whole of God's eternal plan
was found in Christ the Son.

As we partake of Eucharist,
As Christ told us to do,
Remember these eternal words,
"Jesus Christ has died for you."
Dead and buried, He rose again,
With victory o'er the grave;
By His grace, we're not defeated,
To sin no longer slave.

The Bitter Cup

After the supper, His struggle began.
Was fully aware of God's fateful plan.
The man in Him knew just how great the cost.
The God in Him knew the price for the loss.
He knew of the pain—"Please let this cup pass"—
But knew He would do what Father did ask.
The meaning in Hebrew is to pass through,
Not to be released from the things I must do.
The sins of the world no mortal could bear.
Jesus said, "Let's do it to show that we care."
The thought of the Father turning His back
Would be more pain than the stripes on His back.
But knowing the hands that helped drain the cup
Would be the Father's in love lifted up.
Gave Him the joy of enduring the cross,
Embracing the pain to redeem the lost.
Know this, my friend, that the same gift is ours.
The Father helps us in our bitter hours.
He'll never leave us, nor will He forsake.
His grace can never bring forth a mistake.
With that same calm and awareness of love,
We'll know we're covered by our Father's love.
With love comes trusting, with trusting comes faith
That God's in control of trials we face.
When tested and tried, don't walk in despair.
Don't think you're alone with no one to care.
Please rest in the fact that God's got our backs.
We just cannot lose when satan attacks.
So when we're given our own bitter cup,
Look back to Calvary—should help cheer us up.

By fathomless love, the cup has been drained;
Should elicit from us endless refrains.
Refrains of worship of wonder and awe,
Given to Him who is worthy of awe.

Remember the Cross

Remember the supper, remember the cross,
whenever we're tempted or faced with a loss.

A loss being something confronting our will,
to challenge our ego en route to the hill.

On the hill is the cross that we face each day,
where we get to decide our path for the day.

Will we do our own thing and go our own way?
Or choose to serve others to help make their day?

We all know the struggle with great drops of blood
Christ had in the garden, to give of His blood.

He made that decision before—many times.
His Father set boundaries; He stayed in the lines.

He knew Father's purpose; not once did He stray,
ignoring the Father to go His own way.

Now He asks us to walk a life spent for others,
embracing the cross serving our brothers.

As we embrace the cross, we'll not be the same;
the goal of our service, just "in Jesus's name."

Nailed to the Cross

Nailed to the cross—
satan thought he'd won;
he just didn't know
the power of the Son.

Three days later
the price had been paid;
on Sunday morning
Rose from where He laid.

Before He died
He said, "It is done."
Now eternal life
thru Christ had been won.

Eternal life—
how long can that be?
This side of heaven
we just cannot see.

One day we'll know.
When we've run our race,
Jesus will call us;
we'll be face to face.

That glorious day
will never end.
We'll be by His side
and stay there, my friend.

No more of pain
and no more of sorrow.
We'll live in today;
there'll be no tomorrow.

In the Darkness of Night

In the darkness of night,
God hid His own Son
For paying the price,
For things man had done.

The beatings and wounds
He allowed us to see.
Hid the sins of the world
So that we could not see.

All the sins of the world
Would be too much to bear.
It's so hard to deal
With our own little share.

Three full days later,
No bars on the grave,
Jesus came forth
Full of life from the grave.

The battle is over;
The war has been won.
God paid the price
With His own precious Son.

In Remembrance

"Do this in remembrance," He said Thursday night.
Was speaking much deeper than supper that night.

Remembrance is more than a cup and some bread,
Remembrance is doing what Jesus has said.

Spoken with words but much more by the living,
The Master's life—He was constantly giving.

He set the example so that we could see
That living life was not meant for just "me."

He asks us to follow and live like He lived,
Depending on Father for all that He did.

Not even one time did He go His own way.
The Father gave guidance to live day to day.

The thing to remember much more than all else,
That Jesus was willing to give up His self.

He set self aside to honor His father.
When we do the same, He calls us His brother.

We can drink of the cup and eat of the bread,
And not change a thing of the life that is led.

But give of ourselves in serving the Father,
Then we can say the Lord is our brother.

What the supper depicts was not just for "me";
As we do the same, then the whole world will see.

The "supper's" important, but more than the meal,
A life that is giving has special appeal.

An appeal to follow for a world so lost,
The pathway to Jesus goes right through the cross.

The path thru the garden, the trial, the tomb,
The portals of heaven and then the throne room.

Forever and ever, we then will abide
With Jesus our Savior and stay by his side.

Good Friday?

This poem came after a Good Friday service at church, where the focus was on the various events of that day. After the service was over, we were encouraged to leave with a serious attitude, resist talking, and go home. Although the service was very poignant and interesting for me, I was a little disappointed because there was no room for, or mention of, an attitude of rejoicing and being thankful that we can count our blessings for the work of the cross. I'm sure it was a somber and sad night for the original cast, which carried over till Sunday morning. Later, they, too, could look back.

It's only "Good Friday" 'cause we can look back.
The first time it happened, things really looked black.

Their leader'd been tortured; in darkness He'd died.
At the foot of the cross, they knelt down and cried.

By the end of the day, knew all hope was gone.
All their hopes had been dashed; their leader was gone.

He had held such promise: "My kingdom will come."
Finally, freedom from Rome, the feeling of some.

Their vision was narrow, their thinking unclear.
They did not understand His kingdom was near.

The next day despondent, they gave up their wish.
Their dreaming was over. "Come on; let's go fish."

Then came Sunday morning—best news ever heard!
He's risen, He's risen, no longer interred.

They gathered together behind doors for now.
More questions than answers: "What will happen now?"

They didn't believe it. Too good to be true.
Then Christ came among them, said, "Peace be with you."

Then He opened their eyes. Now they understood—
This all had to happen to make Friday "Good."

This was all written down by prophets of old;
The story unfolded, just like it was told.

Now you know the story, how Friday's now "Good."
So get up on your feet, and act like you should.

In the midst of your trial, please never forget.
Sure seems like that Friday—Sunday's not here yet.

So please, please remember when nothing's hummin',
This may be your Friday, but Sunday's comin'.

God's Character

Attributes of Christ in Me

As I look in the mirror,
what is it I see?
I hope it's compassion
looking back at me.
Or is there some kindness
that I can recall,
or maybe gentleness
when someone felt small.
Humbleness should be there
for others to see.
A life like the Savior
should be found in me.
Look harder for patience,
a trial to withstand,
forgiveness to others;
I must take a stand.
Thankfulness tests us.
"Is God in control?"
But thanklessness screams out,
"No, I'm in control."
Most important of all,
it's love we should see.
A life like the Savior
should be found in me.
Constantly checking;
should take time to look.
Is my life reflecting
what's found in the Book?
The life of the Savior,
His attributes seen—
all those attributes
in me, too, should be seen.

With all these together,
the goal of my life,
the attributes of Christ
bring peace and not strife.

Awesome?

Words are the expressions of values we hold.
Some are quite simple, yet some are quite bold.
Some values are constant and never will change,
But some, occasionally, we will rearrange.
There's only one constant that's always the same:
The attributes of God, His holy name.
Much care should be taken when calling His name;
Should only use words expressing that fame.
God is the constant; He will always remain.
His name should never be taken in vain.
With vain meaning common, with no thought of awe,
Where only God's name is worthy of awe.
The writers of old understood with no doubt;
They wrote down God's name, then threw the pen out.
Considered too holy to write common words,
Never again used to write any words.
The awe and respect of these writers of old
Should be used today if the truth were told.
Too oft God's a genie to meet all our needs,
Not a God working on changing our deeds.
Though the curtain was torn that day long ago,
The glory, God's worth, we oft fail to show.
The curtain was torn as to break down a wall
Between God and men, since we took the fall.
The Lord calls us friend if we keep His commands,
But God is still God and honor demands.
We oft use "awesome" to describe many things,
Seldom reserved for the true King of Kings.
Should we use "awesome" to describe common things?
The Bible says "awesome" belongs to the King.

God's Goodness

God's goodness is all around us; it's right before our eyes.
It's not just in the things He's made—the birds, the trees, and skies.

It's more than just our optics that bring things into sight;
It's the Spirit of the Lord that helps us see things right.

We look at the things around us, and oh, they seem so real.
But all these things will pass away. Eternity's what's real.

Our eyes are trained to see the things that we can touch and feel;
When sighted by the spirit, heaven's portal has appeal.

All our lives are but a vapor; real soon this all will pass.
And then we'll see more clearly, like looking thru a glass.

For now we just see partially; our vision's not real clear,
But our vision slowly changes as eternity draws near.

Elisha had a servant boy who thought that they were done;
Elisha prayed, "Open his eyes." He saw the victory won.

But the Syrians couldn't see it, the trouble held in store.
They were camped against Elisha, ready to go to war.

Just like Elisha's servant, too often fail to see
eternity's perspective. Lord, give us sight to see.

When trials of life surround us and we don't know left from right,
Never forget God's Spirit has taken up the fight.

Remind us, Lord, when things seem bad, the story's not complete.
The struggle won't be over till we're sitting at your feet.

Honor and Glory

He's more than insurance to keep us from hell,
So much more than a genie to make all things well.
The God of creation so holy and just,
My friend—honor and glory is truly a must.
He's worthy of worship and honor and praise;
That should be without ceasing for all of our days.
The honor and glory that He's worthy of
should not be reserved Just for heaven above.
We make God too common; we use His name in vain.
We're too often self-centered, treat Him with disdain.
We have this attitude that seems a bit odd.
It's "come into our presence," we want to ask God.
Does God need an invite to be in our midst?
Or was He here before us and we ask amiss?
Could that be arrogance and thoughts filled with pride?
Instead let's be grateful we can walk by His side.
How dare we approach Him with lists of demands?
We just want to keep the control in our hands.
I know God is love in approachable light,
but we'd best come before Him with attitudes right.
Approaching His throne with my hat in my hand,
I wonder if I'll even be able to stand.
The honor that's due Him will bring quite a change.
His glory and honor—will our lives rearrange.
There is a fine line between Lord and friend,
For such a relationship my kingdom must end.
Let's humble ourselves and get down off the throne,
And admit that position should be His alone.

The Mind of Christ

The mind of our Christ—
He came but to serve
And wasn't offended
By people He'd serve.

A need was never
A thing to avoid
But another expression
Of love He employed.

To serve His Father
Was His greatest joy,
Even from the time He
Was just a boy.

From such a young age
The course had been set.
The will of the Father
Must always be met.

So seeking His will
Every day in prayer,
Pleasing His Father was
A constant affair.

The greatest of tasks
He had ever met
Was faced in the garden.
Still, his path was set.

For knowing His Father,
His love it would show.
This obedience was needed;
To the cross He'd go.

So embracing the cross,
He gave up His will.
For love of the Father
Life's blood he would spill.

The Way of Love

It's not my job to change you, to help point out your flaws.
My job is to love you, the second of two laws.

Scripture says the way you love reveals what's in your heart.
If I can't love my neighbor, must find out where to start.

Also says if I can't love those that I can see,
Then the One that I can't see will ne'er be loved by me.

Told to love as we are loved, both by His word and deeds.
His life was an expression of thinking of "their" needs.

In humble resignation, embraced His Father's will.
Spread his arms and took the nails that day on Calvary's hill.

If I'm to live that lesson, then how can I do less?
In humble adoration, it's others I must bless.

Called to consider others to be of greater worth,
Their lives be more important than mine while on this earth.

If I see a brother's need and don't do all I can
To strengthen and encourage, then I don't understand.

I have no understanding of what's been done for me,
Mock the humble sacrifice of Christ for all to see.

If I would be called Christian, the Christ I imitate.
To sacrifice for others, I should not hesitate.

When my life is pondered first, I've not embraced the cross.
And I've yet to surrender and face self's final loss.

Which Christ am I portraying that those around would see,
Who for others spent His life, or just the selfish me?

Trustworthy

"Your ways are not Mine, and it's the same with your thoughts.
Your mind quickly turns to the haves and the have nots.
Your thoughts at first blush, will influence how you feel,
And can easily turn into quite an ordeal.
The reason you struggle—it's a matter of trust.
If you want real peace, you'll find trust is a must.
I've tried to encourage you with promises made;
Keeping your focus on Me, peace never will fade.
If circumstances remove your focus from Me,
You'll be tossed about like the waves on the sea.
My peace will desert you if you take me to task,
If your thoughts start to question the trust that I ask.
The factor that most often will get in the way
Is the fact that you just can't see beyond today.
You can't see the whole picture; you're inside the frame,
But a high level of trust brings glory to My name.
Sometimes I'll use hardship that seems too much to pay;
'Tis for certain, you'll think of a much better way.
Your first inclination is a defensive stance;
The protection of self you just don't like to chance.
But it's those thoughts, dear one, that reveal your doubt,
That I'll give the grace to work it all out.
Your hardships and struggles, designed to rearrange.
In total surrender, your life I will change.
My desire is quite clear in the book of Ez (Ezekiel).
It's that thru all of your struggles, My Lordship you'll see—
Paul wrote in Romans "that it is all for your good."
For My peace will be yours when that truth's understood.
So when life seems in a jumble and all's up in the air,
Remember to trust in My steadfast love and care."

When God Speaks

The God who spoke and the worlds came to be,
this very same God speaks to you and me.

He takes time to say the things we should hear;
obedience will make His presence seem near.

The power of His word is beyond compare;
careful attention will make us aware.

Aware of the life He wants us to live,
total surrender, our own life to give.

He's asked us to serve in all that we do;
blessings toward others will come back to you.

Yet that's not the reason, serve as we do,
but makes the statement "What Christ did for you."

As we live the Word, the message is preached.
The deeds are the seeds; the world can be reached.

Reached for the glory, with Christ lifted up,
so men will be drawn and give their lives up.

No condemnation for those who believe.
Believe in Jesus and pardon receive.

Gift of salvation at such a great cost;
eternal life was won at the cross.

Regrets and Fears

I was regretting the past
and fearing the future;
suddenly my Lord was speaking.
He paused,
I listened,
He continued.

"When you live in the past
with its mistakes and regrets,
it's hard!
I'm not there now;
My name is not I Was.

"When you live in your future,
with worries and fears,
it's hard!
My name is not I Will Be.

"When living in this moment,
Your load will be lighter; I am here.
My grace is sufficient.
My name is . . . I Am."

Grace

Words, Be Careful

Take care, my friend, what words you say.
It could affect another's day.
Not only what but how it's said
Can affect how a life is led.
A gentle word will not bring strife.
A truthful word can save a life.
A harsh word spoken here or there
Could lead a person to despair.
That nursery rhyme from childhood days
Says talk will not affect our ways.
Just know for certain that's not true.
What people say can play on you.
Those sticks and stones may leave their mark,
But spoken words can break a heart.
When Brother James talks of our speech,
His words were meant to warn and teach.
That though the tongue is really small,
Misspoken words can help one fall.
If you would be a godly man,
Then control your tongue and bite it, man.
Be slow to speak and listen hard.
Speak gentle words and be on guard.
When hurtful words come your way,
Be careful what return words say.
A bitter word can start a fight.
Retaliation's just not right.
Be careful, friend, what words you say.
Forgiveness always wins the day.
Our Lord told us to turn the cheek;
Also applies to words we speak.

When others' words bring any hurt,
Don't use words that are short and curt.
The rule of thumb when you reply
Should always be "Give peace a try."
To ne'er return bad same for same
Brings honor to the Savior's name.
Our goal should be our lives be such;
Our lives present the Savior's touch.

The Law That Brought Grace

The law that God gave, set in stone long ago,
Took away the excuse "I didn't know."
It gave us the knowledge of when we go wrong;
The urge to rebel is just way too strong.
'Twas given to see where the benchmark was set;
Perfection's required, that goal can't be met.
The law had established a very high cost;
Unless it was paid, we all would be lost.
The law required that perfect blood must be spilt
Ere relationship with God could be built.
But Jesus obeyed every standard God set,
Thus guaranteeing the price could be met.
When He paid the full price on the cross that day,
Because of that gift, He opened the way.
The curtain was torn from the top to the floor,
Torn by God's hand—not there anymore.
We're able to enter the Most Holy Place,
Now can approach God's throne, by His grace.
Because of that grace, you know it's a free gift,
We can walk by faith, no longer adrift.
Grace, unmerited favor, given in love
Opened the portals of heaven above.
It's only by faith and by His grace alone,
We have the blessing to come to His throne.
We're washed, purified by the blood of God's Son.
We've been justified; sin's curse now is done.
But life has its problems; sometimes we forget.
As long as we're here, He's not finished yet.
He's working to shape us, to be sanctified.
It's part of the process, one day glorified.

Grace Alone Is Enough

Paul laid it all out while stating his case;
The list of worst sinners, he held first place.
But look at my record; I'll make my case.
The best Paul could have is just second place.
Not that I'm bragging or trying to boast,
but checking my list, I'm sure I've the most.
Dreamed I got the chance to sit down and chat.
Knew I could show Paul just where I was at.
As I went down the list, naming each one,
He patiently sat there till I was done.
Instead of rebutting, stating his case,
I watched as a smile crept over his face.
"I've sat here and heard you making your plea,
But why would you want to be worse than me?"
Then for a moment I sat there and cried,
Just realized 'twas because of my pride.
How foolish I felt as it all sank in,
As I realized 'twas proud of my sin.
Then Paul spoke softly; he could have been gruff:
"Remember, my friend, grace alone is enough.
That statement I made about being worst
Was not to compare who's last or who's first.
But rather to show the hope God can give,
To lift your spirit and help you to live.
That hope, the pardon, for you and for me,
That Jesus purchased that day on the tree.
When condemnation gets thrown in your face,
You'll know for sure you're surrounded by grace."
As we rose to go, Paul gave an embrace
And said with a smile, "Be thankful for grace."

Then it was over; the dream seemed so real.
Suddenly, grace, God's gift, had more appeal.
My focus should not be on what I have done,
But the grace I've received, bought by God's Son.

The Gift of Grace

If you want to follow, then take up your cross.
To your life die daily and consider it loss.
It's moment by moment and day after day;
The struggle goes on to give up my own way.
For my flesh is not willing that it should die;
find there are some days I don't even try.
The life I would live, the one I should desire,
Is oft set aside by a rekindled fire.
That "fire of self-will" smolders deep in the heart;
Without resurrection is apt to restart.
But resurrection's elusive till death has occurred,
And death won't happen till the cross we've endured.
There will be a day that plan will be complete,
But until that day, our struggle will repeat.
The gift we've been given, the Spirit within,
Can give us the strength to stand against sin.
That strength is ours when a surrender's in line;
The motive—His will—not entangled by mine.
The more we rely on that unending gift,
The banner of vict'ry you'll find you can lift.
There'll be times of vict'ry, and times that we'll fall.
Please recall, my friend, grace covers it all.
It's only His grace that allows us to stand,
That's freely given by His loving hand.
There might be moments that "fire" will relight.
Might be tempted to say, "By grace it's all right."
Although it is true, because He knows our frame,
To abuse such a gift would be quite a shame.
To esteem so lightly the price that He paid—
My friend, that decision should never be made.

Grace has not been given for us to abuse,
To take for granted, for our pleasures use.
Should that grace be used so that sin can abound?
Paul says, "In our life, sin should never be found!"
Grace was given—salvation's plan to complete,
Was not for the sins that we want to repeat.
Such grace has been given, so we can prepare
For the day His righteous robe we will wear.

Testimonies

I heard your testimony
of how you'd been set free
from the many things you'd done—
envied your soul set free.

Watched as tears streamed down your cheeks,
and heard your voice in praise.
Questioned what was wrong with me—
Don't feel that depth of praise.

We hear great testimonies,
and quickly we compare,
My story doesn't flash like yours—
can lead me to despair.

Wish that mine could be like yours.
I'd have a lot to share.
What convoluted thinking—
Self-pity brings despair.

The thinking in those statements
shows we don't understand.
All was done on our behalf—
gives each the grace to stand.

What we fail to realize,
each story is the same.
All must travel past the cross
to bear that holy name.

Instead, my friend, be thankful
grace spared you from that stuff.
Rejoicing with a brother
should make you glad enough.

Salvation is salvation.
No greater yours than mine.
Every sin that's e'er been done
by grace has been declined.

Justified, Justified

The first thought for this poem was just a single line, "Justified, justified, so hard to believe." I wrote it on a sticky pad and put it on the wall above my desk. I tried several times to push through and complete it, but nothing came. Then one Sunday at church, the message on justification filled in a lot of blanks. I went to work on Monday and don't think I even looked at the note. But then on Tuesday, I put the note on my desk, prayed a little bit, got out a piece of paper, and the Lord gave me the whole poem in less than ten minutes.

Justified, justified;
So hard to believe.
The whole concept rests on Him.

It cannot be paid for;
It cannot be earned.
The whole concept rests on Him.

He has taken our sins,
And He paid the price;
The whole concept rests on Him.

Thru His own precious blood,
We are seen as clean;
The whole concept rests on Him.

His righteousness is ours;
It's on our account.
The whole concept rests on Him.

It's a legal decision,
Not just a nice thought.
The whole concept rests on Him.

It's been chiseled in stone
And cannot be altered.
The whole concept rests on Him.

The Father decided
That's how it would be.
The whole concept rests on Him.

Do you get the picture?
Do you understand?
The whole concept rests on Him.

Justified, justified;
Now I do believe.
The whole concept rests on Him.

It's by His grace alone
We're able to stand.
The whole concept rests on Him.

It's Our Choice

Even when I choose to sin, I find His grace still there.
I know I'll be forgiven, but I still fight with despair,
Because I've grieved the one who died that day for me
And spent His life's blood freely that day on Calvary's tree.
When I commit a sinful act, I treat Him with disdain.
It's like I'm expecting Him to be crucified again.
It was my sin that forced His hand, because He loves me so.
He gave His lone-begotten Son the cost of love to show.
Too often we take lightly the sacrifice He made;
The full redemptive price for us on Jesus Christ was laid.
He chose to follow freely what the Father asked Him to do,
And by His Spirit we can choose to act the same way too.
The deposit of the Spirit, enthroned so deep within,
Will give the strength, if we should choose, to walk away from sin.
It's by our choice we choose to sin; we've no one else to blame.
To turn our face toward righteousness exalts His Holy Name.
I say this oh so often, but it can't be said enough,
"Submit to walk in holiness and avoid the earthly stuff."
That brings us back to grace again; there's naught that we can do,
To earn the right to hear, "Well done; this home's prepared for you."
Ephesians says it's grace thru faith by which we're justified,
Not by works of righteousness but by Jesus crucified.
You see my friend, the gift is free, the price was fully paid.
God sent His Son to pay the price; it was the choice He made.

Image of Grace

The image of grace you see before you,
Though not perfect and with lots of flaws,
One day will stand before God's great throne,
Will be perfect and free from those flaws.

To stand at the throne of the great I Am
Justified, righteous, holy, and clean;
Cleansed by the blood of God's Holy Son,
Like the Lamb, I'll be spotless and clean.

But it's only by grace, not what I do,
That I'll be able to stand on that day.
Robes washed white by the blood of the Lamb,
'Tis by grace, and there's no other way.

Grace is unmerited, cannot be bought;
It will only to be given away.
Given to those who don't deserve it,
Blessings for which there's no way to pay.

The more we try to earn our salvation,
The farther we go into His debt.
Our offerings—putrid—just filthy rags,
Not fit to pay for a sinner's debt.

Grace—Use It or Find It

If you've received grace,
You have to extend it;
You can't keep it all to yourself.

Grace, like all of God's gifts—
Not meant to be hoarded;
They're meant to be given away.

If we cannot give it
To anyone who needs it,
God says that you don't understand.

Impossible to earn,
It's been freely given.
Don't try to make someone earn it.

Don't think you're so special;
You sure couldn't earn it.
So why do you make someone else?

God said, "Forgive them;
They don't know what they've done."
I dare you to try it; it works.

Since He did it for you,
Then do it for others.
It's meant to be given away.

With grace and forgiveness
So closely related,
Give as it's been given to you.

So do unto others
As it's been done to you.
That's how we can show we believe.

If you really struggle
With grace and its giving,
The cross is the place to begin.

The example's been given
By the Father and Son;
The Holy Spirit can teach us

That grace must be given
For every occasion.
As we do, we'll show we believe.

Grace and Grace Alone

It's only by grace and grace alone
Will anyone ever approach the throne.
It will never be by the works we have done;
Fellowship will we enjoy with the Son.
The Father declared, "It's set in stone:
Jesus, the only way to the throne."
Accept the work He did on the cross;
Failure to do so, all will be lost.
"That's too rigid," the world wants to say.
"I want the right to choose my own way."
Walk your own way and find in the end
Eternity forever unpleasant, my friend.
God's the Creator; He made things so.
But lets us choose which way we will go.
He lets us choose; He'll not force His hand,
We have the choice to fall or to stand.
He made the game, and He sets the rules;
Reject the rules and end up as fools.
The only emotion that gets in the way:
"I want the right to choose my own way."
We hold on tight, demanding our rights
Over "our will"; we will choose to fight.
It's from this struggle that God sets us free
From the desire to serve only me.
That's the problem that started it all.
satan said, "I will"—hence came the fall.
We've followed suit since Adam and Eve;
That selfish desire just will not leave.
Jesus came forth, was God's only Son.
When He was done, the victory'd been won.

Saying, "Thy will," He showed us the way;
The very same thing we, too, should say.
Surrender your will to Father above,
Learning to trust His expressions of love.

Only by Grace

You've said we can't earn it.
It's only by grace
that we will be able
to gaze into your face.

It's such a fine balance.
Then what can we do?
The purpose of works
should be centered on you.

It's not for our glory,
or even our fame
that we do our works
just to bolster our name.

All the works that we do
are not done for gain.
They should just be done
to glorify your name.

The glory of the Lord,
as it is revealed,
will draw men to Him,
and their fates will be sealed.

The glory and honor
we give to the Lord
will speak to the world
of the true risen Lord.

The glory that's given
to draw men aside
is the solution
so that we can abide.

To abide in His presence,
surrounded by love,
robed in His glory,
up in heaven above.

Pressing Onward

No, we're not there yet.
There's a long way to go,
but if we press on,
maybe then it will show.

We're not perfect yet,
but we try to take hold.
For the same reason
Christ's taken us to hold.

We must press onward
and then never look back.
Toward the prize straining,
we won't want to look back.

Till the goal is gained
to which God has called us,
we need to live like
the truth that's been shown us.

Oh, to know the Christ
and suffer as He did.
Know His res'rection
and walk the way He did.

For this to happen,
we have to face the cross,
knowing all we've done
becomes a worthless loss.

By faith this happens.
By faith and faith alone.
Resurrection living
with Him around the throne.

The Fountain Within

From deep in the heart our expressions come out.
Those expressions, when spoken, leave us no doubt
as to from which supply our heart tends to speak.
Test your expressions. Are they harsh? Are they meek?
A fountain cannot yield both bitter and sweet,
nor thorns produce any figs for a treat.
The supply that's within will always come out,
and testing will usually bring it about.
The test is usually a challenge of self,
but Jesus says, "Put your self-will on the shelf."
If the fountain within is seasoned by grace,
an angry response just cannot find a place.
If grace is not flooding the fountain within,
then my response might be an expression of sin.
God's grace is sufficient to cover it all.
A proper response could prevent someone's fall.
By showing the grace we've been given in love,
'Twill speak of the love of our Savior above.

Unfathomable Riches

Unfathomable riches—how deep do they go?
This side of heaven, we'll struggle to know.

Not the riches of finance, of glory or fame,
the riches are found in the glory of His name.

The storehouse of heaven, full of His glory,
a search will reveal the crux of the story.

A story of love expressed without measure,
with honor and glory—so much to treasure.

All of the glory of God—ours to behold,
our eyes are opened as His story is told.

When the scales fall off and we're able to see,
then our hearts rejoice as His death sets us free.

The cross with its agony, death, and its pain,
meant to destroy—instead exalted His name.

The name that holds all in the palm of His hand
gives us the grace so that we're able to stand.

It's only by grace, so abundant and free,
the treasures of heaven forever will be.

Hope

Corrected Vision

Your ways, though beyond knowing,
Are right before our eyes.
Too often go unnoticed
'Cause we look thru mortal eyes.

Our eyes of flesh will fail us,
Not disclosing what is real.
Our vision will be clouded,
Trusting then in what we feel.

Just like Elisha's servant
Who thought what he saw was real.
Till Elisha prayed, "Lord show him,
By your Spirit please reveal."

Then once his eyes were opened,
Fear began to disappear.
Eyes now opened, he could see
God's army was mustered near.

Help us, Lord, with eyes of faith
Look beyond what seems so real.
See your hand on our behalf
Before we could make appeal.

To see your hand so clearly
Causes hope to rise within.
The fear with which we're tempted
Flees before it can begin.

With Hope, We Can Rise Above

Like a horse that turns the corner on its way back to the barn,
The rider must pull the reins in so its haste won't cause it harm.
The trail has been long and dusty; the rider weighs upon its back.
But when the welcome turn is made, load seems lighter on its back.
On the ride out from the barn, not known just how far 'twill roam.
But as that turn is recognized, knows it's on its way back home.
The energy that's expended when this hope is realized,
Though much more, it's not a burden—now by hope reenergized.
Of course, the horse is conditioned—it's made this trip before.
It knows that oats and hay will be waiting just inside the door.
Should be same with us, my friend, as we journey through this life;
Since hope gives us a better home, we've God's grace to handle strife.
When struggles that we daily face become the focus of our day,
We've dropped our vision way too low; faith presents a better way.
By faith we know our home's been built on a far and distant shore.
And when salvation's day's revealed, we'll sojourn here no more.
But till that day, know this my friend, all the trials that we face—
They only come to prove our faith and show His amazing grace.
Let the glory of that promised day birth in you a living hope,
And fueled by God's amazing grace, you will have the strength to cope.
The joy that comes from knowing that we're shielded by God's power,
And by the promise of the spirit, you're kept for that very hour.
Like the horse that's turned the corner has just one thought in mind,
By looking toward what's yet to come, 'tis true peace you will find.

Hope

Christ within us, the hope of His glory
speaks to the world a whole different story.
Real hope's not wishing that something will be.
Hoping's true hope when we know it will be.
Fear of the future is nothing to dread.
Real hope is trusting in what God has said;
Real hope has no quiver, for it firmly stands.
Knowing "that hope," we're sustained by God's hands.
Real hope sustains us thru all of our days.
It's real, it's eternal, guiding our ways.
What then can threaten as you make your stand?
When outcomes are held by His almighty hand?
When standing not frightened before our foes
Lets them know it's the start of their woes.
We hope and we pray that things will go right,
And oft get caught in the struggle and fight.
In the midst of your struggle, ne'er forget,
Jesus has said He's not through with us yet.
God's process goes on to make us complete;
Hope realized when we sit at His feet.

Jesus: Hope Realized

I feel like despair has finally set in.
I cry out, "O God!" again and again.
I cry all day long, by night, still no rest.
My eyes fill with tears; at best it's a test.
I feel so forsaken, so all alone.
Is this punishment, my sins to atone?
I've read your promises—"I'll make a way."
But here I still struggle day after day.
Heaven seems to be as solid as brass;
Seems so foreboding, my prayers just won't pass.
Starting to question, "What is it I've done
To cause this silence?" Response? There's just none.
I've prayed, and I've fasted, seeking your face,
In danger of stumbling, losing the race.
My strength is waning. I'm ready to fall,
Tempted to doubt that you're listening at all.
Exhausted, I stopped, no strength left to stand.
'Twas then that I felt your hand take my hand.
Quickly I turned, could not see your face,
But knew I'd been touched by your amazing grace.
Though nothing's yet changed, your peace is in place;
Your promise is there—I'm enabled by grace.
That calm assurance that you'll make a way
Can give the victory o'er struggles each day.
Knowing that you're there is more than enough,
Can cause joy to arise through all of life's stuff.
That hope now restored can grow day by day,
Can give us the strength to trust and obey.

Peace

The Battle

The battle still rages; the war rages on.
The conflict continues; at times, hope seems gone.

But then as I listen with heart and not ears,
I hear Jesus tell me, "Set aside all your fears."

I said, "It is finished," and meant what I said.
"The foe's been defeated; you've nothing to dread."

When walking by sight and not by the Spirit,
Though Jesus is speaking, we just cannot hear it.

Jesus sets the example we all need to see;
To see God as Father, to free you and me.

With the plan set in motion before time began,
The plan's been completed to save sinful man.

The reason we're sinful: we've gone our own way,
Not listening hard to what God has to say.

He gave us free will to do as we please,
He'll not force His hand nor buckle our knees.

He calls us as children with kind, loving words
And guides our steps with His written Word.

He longs to surround us with His loving arms,
Protect us and keep us through all of life's harms.

Spend time in His Word and learn of His ways;
He'll teach you and guide you thru all of your days.

Seven Times or Seventy Times Seven

When Jesus was asked, "How oft to forgive?
How many times should forgiveness I give?"
The question posed—a suggested amount,
"Just how many times? How high should I count?
Should we be gracious and give four plus three?
Just how many times can they offend me?
A qualified number is all that I seek.
Just how many times must I turn my cheek?
How many times must I face their attack
Before it's okay for me to strike back?"
His answer came back without a delay;
His answer would show a whole diff'rent way.
"Do you really think that seven's enough?
For you to lose count would really be tough."
Christ's answer gave a specific amount,
But not a hard number that we should count.
The number He gave—not meant to keep score,
Instead made room to forgive even more.
All that being said, consider this thought:
To count forgiveness the way that we ought.
With a firm number comes limits implied.
Limits were shattered the day Jesus died.
The true love expressed on the cross that day,
Took all of those limits and blew them away.
Forgiveness for us is already there.
Confession, repentance, makes us aware.
Forgiveness is there before we can ask.
When we do likewise, 'twill be quite a task.
Be that as it may, the pattern's the same.
Freely forgive them—the name of the game.

As we've been forgiven, the pattern is real.
Freely forgiven has special appeal.
Since forgiveness comes first, grace on display;
Grace speaks of living a whole diff'rent way.
Grace freely given; it's on our account.
Why should we withhold the slightest amount?
Scripture commands it's the thing we must do.
"Give as freely as has been given to you."
Forgive every time—then counting is done.
If the slate's clean, we'll ne'er reach number one.
Paul in his letter, the "Love Chapter," reads,
Love keeps no record of those wrongful deeds.
If we can't reach one—it's such a far cry
From four hundred ninety—why even try?
To be forgiving in all that they do;
The freedom comes not for them but for you.
"It's finished!" Complete, the process is done.
Forgiveness, no limits, was bought by the Son.
Jesus forgives and remembers no more,
May we do the same and stop keeping score.

Mother's Day

Without our mothers, we'd not even be here.
To know of His presence and that He is near.
We'd never experience His saving grace,
Or ever look forward to seeing His face.
Never experience the love that He shares,
Or feel His compassion and know that He cares.
To know His provision of our daily needs,
Or walk in His strength, when doing good deeds.
Could never experience His peace in a test,
Never know that He always looks for what's best.
Never experience the joy of the Lord
Or hear said, "Well done; come receive your reward."
The wonders of creation we'd never see,
Or ever hold a small child on our knee.
We'd never behold the rising of the sun,
Or even a sunset when each day was done.
I'm sure you know by now, this list could go on,
But then we'd have to stay and be here till dawn.
I've shortened this list with a deference to time,
And I'm finding difficult, more things to rhyme.
So much to give thanks for, not sure where to start,
But, Mother, please know, it's from deep in my heart.
Must stop and say thanks and let you know I care,
For blessings I've received because you were there.
Yet mothers aren't perfect; sometimes let us down.
And sometimes I know, they're not even around.
If you think Mom's failed you, what's been said's still true.
That should be enough for a thank-you from you.
At times, unforgiveness has kept you apart,
But a heartfelt thank-you will soften both hearts.
When all's said and done, by the end of this day,
Be sure to wish your mom a great Mother's Day.

Jonah Got Angry

Jonah got angry when God showed compassion
To Nineveh long, long ago.
He just didn't like it when God relented
Toward people considered his foe.
Jonah got angry and talked back to God.
"I knew that's just what you'd do;
You're full of compassion, quick to forgive.
That's not what I wanted from you.
Those people are wicked, been mean to your kids.
How could you let them get off free?
They'd all be wiped out, utterly destroyed,
If the decision were left up to me.
I ran as far as I could from your plan,
While hoping they would not repent,
But as I expected, when they saw the light,
They surely were quick to repent."
God said to the man, "Why be so angry?
Those people are special to me.
You'd rather die than to show some compassion
To people who're important to me?"
How many times is our quest for justice
Colored in much the same way?
We want them to pay, to pay till it hurts.
God says, "I just don't work that way.
Repentance comes because of my kindness,
Not 'cause I carry a big stick.
I want my children to respond to love
And not from the fear of a stick.
My goal for you is, respond the same way,
Then all those around you will know
The love of the Father is still there for them,
Results from the kindness you show.

Sometimes the response to kindness is slow
And you want to see it right now.
Have patience, my child; I do see the end.
The end's more important than now.
Faith to respond and obey what I ask,
Even without knowing the end,
Will bring forth the day you'll hear me say,
"Come on in—you're welcome home, friend."

Job's Example

Job had a problem—a just, righteous man.
satan was angry, and he had a plan.
satan said, "Give me the power to destroy,
And I will disrupt your true pride and joy."
God gave permission to try out his plan
And said, "You are wrong; he's my kind of man."
"He'll curse you and hate you," he said with a grin.
God said, "I doubt it. Let his test begin."
satan brought trouble and pain and sorrow,
Then he gloated, "He'll curse you tomorrow."
Tomorrow arrived, and Job still stood true
And boldly stated, "I'll never curse you."
"You've won the first round," satan said with a frown.
"Just one more shot, and I'll bring him down."
Given permission, he planned so much strife.
"Just one condition: you can't take his life."
Covered with sores from his head to his feet,
Try as he might he could not bring defeat.
Most of us know the rest of the story.
Job stood the test, and God got the glory.
In our lives today, the same thing applies;
God's in control of all of our lives.
Going thru problems we don't understand,
Have faith, my friend; He's holding your hand.
He won't disappear; He'll not turn His back
Or leave you alone when satan attacks.
Trials seem lonely, with no one to care.
Please don't give up and live in despair.
With promises given, the list is so long;
Learn them, my friend, and you'll never go wrong.

"Leave nor forsake, I never will do,
Is one of the best I've given to you."
Please learn then from Job, whatever you're in.
Giving glory to God will keep you from sin.
Your plight may not end this side of the grave,
But He'll give the strength to trust and be brave.
Job said it, my friend, not just one time but twice,
"Give glory to God; the peace will be nice."

Hard to Forgive

It's not how we're treated that should rule our day.
We should be accepting of God's perfect way.

God says, "Be forgiving, no matter the cost."
So be just like Jesus and pick up your cross.

"Please, Father, forgive them"—we've all heard it said.
Forgiveness—not easy when self is not dead.

We say repentance should always come first.
God says that repentance comes second, not first.

You know, "vengeance is mine" is what the Lord said.
Forgiveness won't happen when egos are fed.

The Lord hung on a cross to show us the way.
Forgiveness can happen when we choose His way.

There are no exceptions; the method's the same.
Forgiving each other exalts Jesus's name.

Forgiving a brother can be a real test
To see if we're dead yet or think we're the best.

But it's not just our brother we need to forgive.
Forgiveness for all if like Jesus we'd live.

In the midst of it all, put a smile on your face.
Shows what it's like to be surrounded by grace.

From Cloudy to Peace—What a Gift!

Dark and foreboding, the clouds had rolled in,
Gave a bleak outlook ere the day could begin.
I had tossed and turned all night long on my bed;
The fear of the unknown had filled me with dread.
My thoughts had turned to what the day held in store.
The way it stacked up, couldn't handle much more.
The worries and troubles I had focused on
Stirred up the pot through the night before dawn.
Thoughts of despair, like shoes made out of lead,
Stopped me from moving, could not clear my head.
I thought as I lay there, "Dude, shake these thoughts loose;
For the tasks of the day, you won't be much use."
As I slowly sat up, my feet hit the floor;
The Lord brought to mind Scriptures I'd read before.
For the journey through troubles, He'd show the way.
That a fresh batch of mercy—new every day.
I'll never forsake you or leave you alone.
The light for your pathway to you will be shown.
To the right or the left, I'll show you the way.
With faith as your guide, you can hear what I say.
For all of the struggles, grace will make a way.
So you can rejoice at the end of the day.
Cast your burdens on Him, for He will sustain;
Won't let you be shaken, even when in pain.
As I sat there pond'ring each verse brought to mind,
The clouds began lifting—knew peace I would find!
Now focused on promises, bolstered by hope,
I knew with the trials of the day I could cope.
The day's now completed, sat down to review,
Gave thanks for the grace that helped me make it through.

My burdens He'd carry if left at his feet,
Now has more meaning as the day is complete.
The strength I experienced was not my own;
My surrender, by faith, brought power from the throne.
Lord, help me remember the thoughts of today.
With your help, can live a whole diff'rent way.
To be just like Jesus asleep on the sea,
A life full of peace will be your gift to me.

Forgiveness—A Standard

When I make mistakes and it comes to the light,
I defend myself to avoid what's right.

When I should repent and fall on my knees,
Admit that I'm wrong; I do as I please.

The standard is clear, yet I choose to fight,
making up reasons to defend my rights.

It's wrong or it's right; there are no shades of gray.
Absolute standards I need to obey.

Instead I reason and come up with ways
To keep from going the godly, right way.

Forgiveness, my friend, is a two-way street,
To be received and given—both are sweet.

We're asked to forgive and do it with love,
Without conditions, like we're done—with love.

Like Jesus himself forgave from the cross,
The only way we can is to pick up our cross.

Our Master forgave from the cross, we know.
"Father, forgive them; they really don't know."

Like Jesus forgave from the cross that day;
If I'd be like Jesus, there's no other way.

Unlimited grace—it's so hard to give,
Yet that's how Jesus has asked us to live.

It's hard to forgive when we know there's a chance
'Twill happen again. I must take that chance.

'Twill only happen with grace from above,
Then my expressions will speak of His love.

Sermonettes

New Address—Please Forward

It all stayed the same for so many years.
Grew quite accustomed, no need to shift gears.
The prospect to move and start a new life;
So many questions—it brought so much strife.
What must I give up? How much will it change?
How much of my life must I rearrange?
I'd been there so long. Did I want to move?
I thought my life had a comfortable groove.
Could navigate around things that were tough.
I found great comfort in all of my stuff.
If I just ignored things, thought they'd go away.
Maybe I'd deal with it some other day.
Was really enjoying my life of ease;
I answered to no one, could do as I please.
What would my friends think? What would they say
If I made this change by moving away?
Talked to my friends, asked them, "What should I do?
What would you do if it were left up to you?"
Some told me, "Try it; life oft takes a turn.
If you don't like it, can always return."
Others said, "No! It would be a mistake.
Don't take a chance with the choices you make."
Received their input; intentions were good.
The struggle was mine; that I understood.
Then came this letter. I read what it said;
A lot of the words were written in red.
Spoke of a home that was being prepared,
A special project by someone who cared.
It spoke of a debt that had to be paid
And how by one life that purchase was made.
It spoke of a love beyond all measure.
'Twas spent for me, a gift I should treasure.

It spoke of the state that my soul was in.
It told me my heart was tarnished by sin.
The message was clear—I needed to move;
Change the goals of my life and find a new groove.
But how could I do it? Give this all up?
Even though my life was an old, empty cup.
To receive this gift of love that was spent,
Had to believe and then also repent.
I wanted to do it, but oh what a price.
Before I could do it, I counted it twice.
Total surrender was what I understood.
The works I could do amount to no good.
'Twas naught I could do this position to gain,
But accept that gift of love through the pain.
I made the decision, made in cold blood;
A new sense of peace came on like a flood.
A burden lifted; just was not aware
Of how much I carried—so much despair.
An new outlook on life felt in my heart,
Oh so thankful for a brand-new start.
In joyful surrender, I picked up my cross,
Said goodbye to this world—considered it loss.
One other thing in the letter was plain:
The world might be loss, but heaven I'd gain.
The move now was made—the transfer complete!
Please forward mail to "The Great Mercy Seat."

Motives for Prayer

Lord, give me some time, and I'll lay it all out,
So I can explain what I'm talking about.
You see, I've got this list that needs to get filled.
I want you to know what it is I have willed.
It says in your book, if by faith I believe,
Whatever I've asked for, that I will receive.
If I ask in your name whenever I pray,
You've promised to give me whatever I say.
I'm sure that my faith is sure to impress;
With the verses I quote, you can't help but bless.
I've picked out these verses; your Word's always true.
It's a really long list; it's not just a few.
My faith is the focus that brings things about.
Just have to speak it, believe and not doubt.
My words are the force by which faith is driven;
If I do it right, my blessings are given.
Isn't that right?

What gives us the right to tell God what to do,
With the focus completely centered on you?
How pompous of us to try to persuade,
To usurp God's will and the plans He has made.

My friend, give me a moment to share some insight.
We must read all Scripture to see all things right.
If this is your prayer life, your focus is wrong.
All the focus on "me" just does not belong.
My friend, let's read all the verses on prayer.
To the need for a change, you will become aware.
Read not just the verse but the text on each side,
To get the whole story and your eyes opened wide.
The Scriptures list reasons why prayers are not heard,
With most summed up well in James 4 of God's Word.

James gives us instructions of how not to pray.
Our focus should not be to have our own way.
God says He'll not answer our self-centered prayers,
But asks us to focus on others' affairs.

The disciples asked Jesus, "Teach us to pray,
So when we ask Abba, we'll know the right way.
We've watched you in prayer and have seen that God hears,
And at times even seen your cheeks wet with tears."
He first gave them a list of what not to do.
"Don't let this behavior be bound up in you."
Then He said, "Brothers, this is how you should pray;
It'll help you to pray the way that I pray.
Father, your name is hallowed; please give me your ear.
My request is simple: bring your kingdom near.
I want your will to be utmost in my life,
That you'd receive glory and honor, not strife.
Ask for daily bread and with that be content;
To seek more than that, you might have to repent.
You must ask forgiveness be given to you,
The same way forgiveness is given by you.
Don't let us be tempted to do what is wrong,
And keep us away from our foe that is strong.
To sum this all up, that it not take too long,
To pray other than that, my friend, is just wrong.
Be sure your petitions don't make a demand
When approaching the throne, if you want to stand.
Please humble yourself when approaching the throne
To state your requests and to let them be known.
There's one more attitude that's high on the list
Of how we should pray and not get your prayers "missed."
A thankful heart should accompany your prayers.
'Twill acknowledge the One who knows all your cares.
A thankful heart is an expression of trust,
To walk in God's peace then, my friend, it's a must.

"It's Only a Test"

"It's only a test," my mother would say
when faced with a difficult trial.
"Don't ever forget that this, too, shall pass,"
she often would say with a smile.
The way that she looked at all of her trials
was usually not a big deal.
For years and years, she had trusted the Lord.
Never failed to provide a meal.
We never went hungry, always had clothes;
the roof kept us all warm and dry.
We didn't know that the cupboard was bare,
so "Thank you, Lord," was our reply.
Then many years later, after I had grown,
and was facing my own set of trials,
I remembered what Mom had said.
"Let God be your strength in your trials.
And don't lean on your own understanding.
Just trust in the Lord, day by day.
He's promised to never forsake you;
He'll guide you and show you the way."
As the years went by and Mother grew old,
she longed for the day she could leave.
Meet with her loved ones and all the saints,
but to her Savior she'd cleave.
Sometimes she'd complain, "Lord, why am I here?
I'm tired and I just want to rest."
Then came the chance to remind her with
"But, Mom, this is only a test.
Don't ever forget that this, too, shall pass;
real soon all your struggles will end.
That day will come. You'll walk down the streets
with Jesus, your Savior and Friend."

Her school days are done. There'll be no more tests;
she's finally home with her Lord.
I'm sure she heard as she entered in,
"Well done. Come receive your reward."
What's left for me as I now carry on?
Remember and never forget
that God said He'd supply all our needs,
and He's not failed anyone yet.
And now it's my turn to pass this along
and teach it to all that I may.
That trusting the Lord thru all of your trials,
He will get you thru every day.
Many years from now, as my kids look back,
reflect on the life that I led,
pray that they'll see me faithful as she
and recall the lessons I said.
I have to trust that I did some things right
and leave the results to the Lord.
And hopefully hear as I enter in,
"Well done. Come receive your reward."

Good and Bad Redefined

The premise from which this poem came to be:
"That God's in control of more than we see."
God tells us His thoughts we can't comprehend;
He asks us to trust Him right to the end.
Today's discussion of what's bad or good,
Hopefully helps us to think as we should.
Not meant to deny that evil exists,
Instructed by God, we must resist.
If evil's not there, of armor no need;
Issued by the Spirit, we'd better take heed.

What's good or bad? Who gets to decide
Just where, when, or how that peace will abide?
God said from the start, "That choice is mine;
Leave that tree alone, or there'll be a fine.
This garden is yours and all it contains,
Except of that fruit, I tell you refrain.
If you eat that fruit, I promise you'll die."
satan spoke up, said, "You'll die? That's a lie."
Another temptation: "Like God you will be.
Go ahead, partake; you'll be able to see."
We fell to temptation, ate the fruit of the tree;
We didn't resist—"It looked good to me."
We were not willing to simply obey.
Expelled from the garden, now on our own way.
Now back to the top, the question at hand:
Who gets to decide? Where do you stand?
Before a quick answer, here's some food for thought.
Some you have thought of, some possibly not.
Jesus was teaching; the man called Him good,
Cautioned by Jesus to think as he should.
"God alone is good" was Jesus's reply;

Equal with God, Jesus did not deny.
God can't be tempted or have evil thought.
His intentions all good; evil they're not.
Another deception, though subtle at best:
"How can God be good, with life such a test?
Too often, my friend, this thought has prevailed:
"If my life has troubles, Jesus has failed."
Has not God promised us peaches and cream?
When troubles arise, it destroys the dream.
So what do we do with things we deem bad?
Do we just move on, or think we've been had?
(By move on I mean have faith and not doubt,
That in the end good will be worked out).
Have you learned to rejoice when things are tough?
Or think God has failed to protect you enough?
Now here's a challenge to think as you should.
All circumstances are gathered for good.
For those who are called as God has ordained,
The good He intended will always retain.
If God's purpose—to fulfill what is good—
Causes a change in our thinking, it should!
God's plan's to prosper and not bring us harm.
He's able to guide by His mighty arm.
If all that happens, by God's been designed,
Our knowledge of good must be redefined.
If we define good as what pleases me,
Good's more complicated than just what I see.
Now here's a thought process few want to address.
Some understanding would end lots of stress.
Is God by nature inherently good?
Would He do evil? Even if He could?
I'm sure you'd agree the answer is no.
He'd be conflicted, division would show.
A house that's divided will never last,
Not looking forward or back to the past.
Now comes the hard part; it might rock your boat.
It's somewhat diff'rent, not quoted in rote.
If God writes the story, beginning to end,
What in daily life could be bad, my friend?

What we deem as bad, betwixt you and me,
Is only because we ate of the tree.
'Twas in rebellion that we ate the fruit,
Took rights to condemn what does not suit.
If "all" works for good as we've read before,
Then what we call bad, we should not ignore.
Throughout the Scripture, time after time,
God uses trouble His will to refine.
What we think is bad, God uses for good.
A thankful heart will think as it should.
It's part of the process God's working out.
That makes it good, yet our flesh wants to doubt.
With all this in mind, too often our choice
Is grumble again and not to rejoice.
Let's reason together a minute or two.
How should we respond to things we go through?
First let's consider before we proceed,
The source of our trials, the hope that we need.
Do we firmly believe God is in charge,
That there are no outside forces at large?
Free-roaming radicals, free from control,
Do as they please, from all exact a toll.
Do we believe all's allowed by His hand,
And His promised strength, all to withstand?
If we know God's good, His plans we can trust.
Should make the goal of rejoicing's a must.
Told to rejoice and give thanks in all things,
Praise Him for the peace and the blessings it brings.
To walk as content in fellowship sweet,
Can be like the day we'll be at His feet
To close this all up and bring to an end.
Please, please, consider this caution, my friend.
To grumble and gripe at the King of Kings,
When all that He's done and all that He brings,
Seems like a bit on the blasphemous side.
And 'twill never allow that peace to reside.
Salvation's not threatened, but why'd we deny
Sweet fellowship with a grumbling reply?
That fruit can't be returned back to the tree,

We can't go back to the garden, you see.
There will be a day perfection returns.
The peace and the joy for which our heart yearns.
But until that day, God still longs to hear
Our hearts rejoicing in praises so clear.
Listen to Paul; he states time after time,
No matter the fix, rejoicing's in line.
Beaten, adrift, stoned, thought it no loss,
In light of knowing God's power of the cross.
May we, too, be aware of the same thing—
The knowledge of God, the peace that it brings.

Footprints—A Closer Look

Have you read the poem called "Footprints" yet?
It speaks of when we feel all alone.
We're so sure that we've been abandoned
'Cause there's just one set of footprints shown.
But as those lines lovingly express
The one set of footprints that we see—
They are not ours, but God's alone
Because He's carrying you and me.
But if we would examine closely
The line of footprints that we see,
There, in each footprint that's left behind,
There is a graphic we all can see.
But unlike a tire leaving tread marks,
Which are erased by the wind and rain,
The graphic seen in those footprints
Is perm'nent—forever will remain.
With even closer observation,
We'll see details overlooked before.
Some prints seem to have a shall'wer depth,
While others appear to have much more.
The reason some prints have different depths
Is not the varied softness of the sand,
But the factor that determines depth
Is increased weight carried in His hands.
It's about time to solve this riddle.
What's seen in the footprints in the sand?
The second part of the questions asks,
"What is the weight carried in His hand?"

The first question's answer:

We don't need to use a special glass.
The graphic seen there reveals His care.

'Tis the signature of the Master.
It's not but "grace" that's written there.

The second question's answer:

The cause of the deeper impressions—
another expression of the same.
It's God's grace in greater measure,
To give strength and glorify His name.
Scripture says we'll never comprehend
Or have understanding of His ways.
That the grace and mercy that we need
Will be given freely all our days.
For the countless souls He's carried,
His grace was never in short supply.
So explain to me why grateful
Is not our constant and first reply?
With such acknowledged testimonies
And all the promises written there.
What is it that rises within us
Causing us to doubt and to despair?
Could it be the faith we've talked about,
That we've proclaimed from the very start,
Has failed to travel the full distance?
The eighteen inches from head to heart?
'Twas completed—He said, "It's finished"
that day he died on Calvary's tree.
The full price was paid to ransom us
To set each and every captive free.
So if tempted to feel abandoned,
And before our doubts and fears can start,

Remember this promise:

The grace that brought salvation
Resides forever within our heart!
When needing strength to brave the struggle
And want the smile to stay on your face,
The wherewithal to keep rejoicing
'Twill be provided by Amazing Grace.

Evidence versus Theory = Need a Savior?

When pulling some weeds in the garden one day,
As I picked up a rock, I heard the Lord say,
"Why do you marvel so at things that are old?
Have you considered that small rock that you hold?
Of the things that man makes, they'll all fall apart;
That rock that you hold has been here from the start.
From the very first day, that rock has been here.
True contemplation will bring my presence near.
But yet there are those who say I had no part;
A swamp-spawned amoeba was really the start.
That all seen around you just happened by chance.
Without any proof, that's a difficult stance.
You only have theories with no real hard facts.
Can't explain away my miraculous acts.
The push to say all things just came to be
Is just man's attempt at not dealing with Me.
If you look away and pretend I'm not real,
You can do what you want; it's not a big deal.
There'll be no absolutes, if no one's in charge;
Eventually chaos will loom very large.
I'm not being arrogant; I wrote the rules.
Without strict adherence, you'll end up as fools.
Because of My standards, perfection demands.
Just one little slip, and your life's in My hands.
But you say, "Perfection, that's just not fair."
Just read farther on, and it will clear the air.
You see, I've made provision, only one plan
To restore fellowship forever with man.
I've chosen a sacrifice spotless and clean
That'll cover your sins so they just won't be seen.

The sacrifice—Jesus, my own special Son,
Has paid the price for the sins man has done.
If sin's score was kept, only zeros would do.
A score of one says there's no hope for you.
What I'm trying to say is, you'll all fail the test.
Your need of a Savior—not just a jest.
I gave you a choice, which way you should go,
Back in the garden so long, long ago.
Today the same question as asked way back then,
Will each of you choose to follow the trend?
The trend to go just the way you desire.
It seems to be an unquenchable fire.
There is a way to extinguish the blaze
And set yourself free for all of your days.
Set free from the struggle of satan of old,
Shackled by pride and being real bold.
He said, "I'm good enough; I'll make my own way.
I'll be just like God and rule my own day."
Instead, look to the cross, the work that was done.
The sacrificed life of Jesus, My Son.
Not even one time did He go His own way,
But yielded His will, said, 'I will obey.'
He went to the cross—what a glorious feat!
A life spent for others; the plan's complete.
The plan justifies the cost to you—nil.
'Twas stamped Paid in Full that day on the hill.
The only thing needed for you to receive:
Acknowledge your need, then truly believe.
There will come a day when every knee will bow,
I'd rather see you start practicing now."

Does Anyone Care?

Royalty passes; the road lined by the throngs.
The thought in their heart: "How will they right the wrongs?"
The motorcade passes; they're now out of sight.
What hope do you have? They're aware of your plight.
When all's said and done and they've gone down the road,
How good do you feel that they'll lighten your load?
Have you taken comfort your troubles will change?
The struggles you have will somehow rearrange?
The struggle's continual, day after day;
Self-preservation consumes much of our day.
Look toward the future for the light at the end;
Hope starts to fade—we just see darkness, my friend.
Before you give up and get filled with despair,
There is an answer—One who truly does care.

Old prophecies spoke of a day yet to come.
A deliv'rer would come for all, not just for some.
At just the right time, this new "Royal" was born.
Our hopes were awakened on that Christmas morn.
Heralded as peaceful, a new way of life,
A whole diff'rent way of now dealing with strife.
Mostly unnoticed, no parade passing by,
This new "Royal" had a diff'rent reply.
"I'm not passing by; my intention's to stay,
Teaching you how to live a whole diff'rent way."
This new life is diff'rent; our focus should change.
This new Royal's law will at first seem so strange.
The first point of focus is love for the Lord,
And then our love for others, we must afford.
"So you must surrender and let me move in;
My promise is more than just freedom from sin.

But before that promise, you must understand.
I'll be in charge; you won't be lending a hand.
On the throne of your heart, there's no room for two.
There'll be no partnership; it's me or it's you.
You can't serve two masters; on that I've been clear.
You'll reject the one; hold the other one dear.
It must be full surrender without reserve;
Resigning all self your Savior to serve.
Your will and my will are like water and oil.
They'll never combine; they'll always recoil.
I know it's a struggle for you to let go,
To surrender your life to what you don't know.
It's not a matter of knowing what or who;
The issue is trusting what I have told you.
If you want the truth, it must be understood—
My intentions for you are nothing but good.
Struggles that continue are controlled, don't you see.
They're designed to keep you trusting in me.
It's my Spirit working, within and without.
As cause and effect to bring my will about."

Now back to the promise; 'twas mentioned before.
There's freedom from sin, but there's oh so much more.
The vict'ries you long for, the peace that you crave,
Can work in full measure your side of the grave.
The way that I call you to walk free from strife
will only be yours through a res'rected life.
But ere resurrection there comes quite a cost.
It's called death to yourself; consider it lost.
And that is the freedom, no longer a slave,
To be free from self and the things that you crave.
Set free to serve others as unto the Lord.
"Well done, faithful servant" will be your reward.
What more could we ask for? But still it's a choice.
With that realization should not but rejoice.

Depression

Please hear me completely; please hear what I say
Before you get angry and throw this away.
My goal's not to hurt you or make you get mad,
But hopefully show you the way to be glad.

Please pause for a moment; don't be so intense.
Just hear what I say; please take no offense.
Before passing judgment, please hear what I say.
I'm not trying to judge, but just help your day.

Depression's a battle we all have to face;
When we succumb, we've pulled out of the race,
The race that God's called us to strive as to win.
My friend, don't give up, for God calls it sin.

Depression's a heartache that ties us in knots
And usually influences all of our thoughts.
It keeps us from doing what we should do;
Will keep me from being friendly with you.

"But you don't understand," we're all prone to say.
"It's because I'm a victim I feel this way.
Life's events have been bitter; been hurt a lot.
The whole world's against me; I'm sure it's a plot."

The more it continues, the deeper the hole,
Escape will get harder, will take quite a toll.
Emotions all jumbled and heart filled with strife;
If left uncorrected, we might take our life.

When the hole is deep and the pile seems too high,
We too often give up and won't even try.
With just one thought of thanks, we can turn the tide,
And we'll find that God's peace will surely abide.

Before I go farther, something I must say.
We won't live forever; we're wasting away.
There will be some failures and struggles in life;
the way we respond brings contentment or strife.

Our response will speak of our level of trust.
If God's in control, then our thanks is a must.
God has told us all His intentions are good.
Don't be discouraged; give thanks like you should.

The hook in depression is "focus on me."
When Jesus's instructions are "focus on Me!"
He lovingly asks us to trust and not doubt.
He knows the ending and will work it all out.

Over and over God's Word's so very clear.
If you count your blessings, then peace will draw near.
A thankful heart keeps us in tune with his plan.
Then our confession is "I'm safe in His hand."

I know this isn't pop'lar. I've said it before,
Not getting depressed can be quite a chore.
But so many times, it's really by choice
That depression stops us from hearing God's voice.

I know there are many who give a way out,
Say, "An imbalance is the reason, no doubt."
The source of imbalance they rarely will know,
But treat it they must, their compassion to show.

They have good intentions, we all know for sure.
But often don't speak of the absolute cure.
Medications are given to help our malaise,
To help us feel better and comfort our days.

There is a full treatment we all need to find.
Can end our depression and give a clear mind.
It's really quite simple, but can take some time
To change our thought process and make His will mine.

This one little phrase can change our direction,
Help our thoughts change and end our depression.
This one little phrase that God asks us to say
Is "Thank you, Lord Jesus; I'll trust you today."

"Thank you" acknowledges that God's in control,
And trusting in Him will bring peace to your soul.
"Thank you" is behavior God asks us to live,
A visible statement of trust we should give.

It's not only depression but negative thoughts
That will tie your spirit in a mass of knots.
Try not to forget when those thoughts try to start.
They just won't find a place in a thankful heart.

The heart of thanksgiving that's filled wall to wall
Has no place to harbor those wrong thoughts at all.
With those thoughts taken care of, your joy will be shown;
can give them a desire to approach the throne.

Deception: So Subtle

There is no record of reaction that night,
The news that Messiah had burst into sight.
If what the shepherds had reported was true,
'Twould be great news for a Jerusalem Jew.
I'm sure some went along, the truth to observe,
To see for themselves of this "king" who would serve.
To just serve their desires, to free them from Rome,
To send them all packing away from their home.
Upon their arrival, hope turned to forlorn.
How could this new king in a manger be born?
I'm sure word spread quickly: "The rumor's not true;
This 'king' that's been born will do nothing for you."
Because of their feelings, "what's in it for us?"
Their eyes had been blinded; they continued to fuss.
Now as we read the story time after time,
Always say to ourselves, "Why were they so blind?
Why couldn't they see that Messiah was here,
Fulfilling the Word to bring His kingdom near?"
The kingdom they looked for was the earthly kind,
To make their life easy, both body and mind.
They read past the promise; the kingdom He'd bring
Would be brought about by a suffering king.
Because they looked past what the prophets foretold,
Their own expectations then actually took hold.
It became their truth as to how it should be.
Be cautious, my friend; that could be you and me.
If we're not careful, we do much the same thing.
We're oft not aware what His kingdom will bring.
We have the same problem; the struggle's the same,
Our self gets in the way, won't glorify His name.

We form expectations of how things should be
But find tunnel vision can blind you and me.
We look so intently at things as we choose;
We, too, can miss events that God plans to use.
We can't pick just one verse and hold on real tight.
It's God's whole council that will shed the right light.
We know that a truth can be twisted around,
To say however we might want it to sound.
Every aberrant group will point to one verse
To help make their point—oh, how they rehearse.
But the rest of their text is riddled with errors,
So flee them, my friend, like you would your night terrors.
My warning to us is to not be deceived—
Thru cunning and logic or words we receive.
Be like the Bereans and test all we hear
To grasp all the truth, not just tickle your ear.
I've said this before, and I say it again,
The reason we struggle is the self within.
The self that's within is our number one foe.
It's the fountain from which all other sins flow.
For every sin that we will ever perform
Comes from choosing "my" way and treating it as norm.
'Twill reveal itself in myriad of ways.
Our fierce rebellion will always trouble our days.
It's time to repent, laying all self aside.
Make room for the Spirit so He can abide.
Can't be two masters on the throne of our heart—
For us to step down is a good place to start.
The Word's very clear that two masters won't do;
The failure to choose will bring unrest to you.
Of the two masters who contend for the throne,
Be honest, my friend—to which one are you prone?
We've been drawn by the Spirit to come to the cross,
But we hesitate 'cause we think there'll be loss.

But then in the end, as the story is read,
If we'd be like Christ, we have to be dead.
But that will not happen until we believe
That being dead in Christ, new life we receive.
When we're dead in Christ, the world has no sway.
Though satan may buffet, God's will rules the day.
As we learn to die, as each day goes along,
In service to Jesus, He gives a new song.
The song of salvation will rise from within
And ring from the rafters as praises begin.

Curse or Blessing?

Some days are good and some are bad.
And then some seem even worse.
On those that seem so very hard
We're sure that it's a curse.
We like it when our day goes smooth;
We feel freedom from despair.
But when the day is really tough,
We're convinced there's no repair.
When we look at circumstances
And let them affect our day,
Then we're not looking to the Lord.
We forget God makes each day,
Not just the hours twixt twelve two times,
But each moment in between;
For God controls each moment
That His glory might be seen.
If our trials overwhelm us
And we're sure that all is lost,
Remember God's plans for our good,
And that good had quite a cost.
We can find throughout the Scriptures
Difficulties have a place.
Trials bring a perseverance
Lives of ease cannot replace.
We're familiar with the story
Of a man of God named Job,
Whom God allowed satan to test.
Afflicted, he tore his robe.
As he sat in dust and ashes,
In his heart of hearts he knew
The sovereignty of God was real;
What he saw might not be true.

Though he did not understand it,
Thought how he'd lived was right.
The truth of God he'd lived by
Didn't balance with his plight.
Now in spite of all his troubles
Job refused to just give in.
Refused to curse the God he loved,
Did not enter into sin.
Even though Job did gripe a bit,
'Twas because he was confused.
He thought a life lived for the Lord
Would prevent being abused.
By spending time to read God's word,
You'll know that isn't so.
Our trials help to strengthen us
And Christ's attributes to grow.
Now just like Job, who didn't know
What went on behind the scene,
We too can learn to walk the same;
What is real might not be seen.
God says true sight is spiritual;
What our eyes see, not so much.
The spirit sees eternal things;
What our eyes see, we can touch.
So when trials of life surround us
And we're tempted to despair,
And just can't see the end in sight,
Don't think He doesn't care.
God says each test has a purpose
Through which we're designed to grow,
To grow in the knowledge of His grace
And the sovereign Lord to know.
So when your trials surround you,
Rejoice; stand to your feet.

A thankful heart shows satan
Another moment of defeat.
Now back to Job—one final thought:
O'er all, his attitude expressed,
He praised the Lord for who He was,
Whether he felt cursed or blessed.
Though He slay me I'll still trust Him,
Was Job's most apt reply.
When our actions just like his,
God's sovereignty won't deny.
God is sovereign, the King of Kings,
Though His purpose oft not known.
As we can trust all that He does,
His great glory will be shown.

An Unlimited Pass

Completed after a trip to the ER:
Let's think of it this way; in our world today,
A pass is a "freebie" for which you don't pay.
A sought-after item—considered a score,
If we get one once, we'd sure like to get more.
These passes are fleeting; too soon they are o'er.
As you're walking away, they're locking the door.
God, too, gives out passes, but He does it right.
Of the ones that He gives, there's no end in sight.
Let's recap a story to help state my case.
With clear understanding might keep it in place.

Years ago, a chorus that we sang a lot,
"I Will Enter His Gates," was really quite hot.
It spoke of our thanks, also spoke of our praise
We should be expressing for all of our days.
The words came from a psalm that King David wrote,
Though the first words sung, not a perfect quote.
The words as we sang them started with "I will . . ."
The words David wrote—a command to fulfill.
Now the words as we sang them right from the start—
Bold declarations, the intent of our heart.
Consider caref'ly what has happened before,
When some hearts that were grumbling knocked on the door.
The children of Israel, tough times in the sand,
Paid a high price when grumbling got out of hand.
Not far into the trek, the grumbling did start;
They could not a find a thankful place in their heart.
Backed up to the Red Sea without any boat,
With a puff of wind, it became a dry moat.
The wind stopped blowing. water came rushing back.
The Egyptians all drowned—no fear of attack.

No more slave labor or bricks made without straw;
Daily manna, then quail got stuck in their craw.
When water was needed, came straight from a rock;
Of all God's provisions, they never took stock.
For all God's provision, no thankful reply.
All they chose to do was to grumble and cry.
Fin'ly, the threshold of God's promised home,
Best part of the promise, they'd nevermore roam.
Though God gave the promise, their hearts filled with doubt.
The giants, too big. "God, you can't work this out!"
Because of their failure to trust what God said,
Forty years in the sand, most all of them dead.
God called it "contempt"; they ten times failed the test.
With a grumbling heart, they were banned from His rest.
The challenge for us who are living today—
We've got to take care we don't act the same way.
Today's no diff'rent, the "rest" not quite the same.
Our "rest" for today is "at peace" in His name.
If they had only said thanks a time or two,
More might have entered, much more than just two.
Remember Queen Esther approaching the king,
Knew without approval her death it would bring.
As Ahaserus honored Esther's approach,
we need that honor not to earn a reproach.
I'm not trying to say that a grumbling heart
Will make this life end and eternity start,
Nor eliminate from us an urgent plea,
Always leaving room for a plea to be free.
But like those born again, with the gifts that ensue,
Our hearts should always be saying "Thank you."
But if I seek audience to make my request,
Has my heart been prepared? Will it pass the test?

Does my heart acknowledge the grace God supplied
That was imparted to us the day Jesus died?
The full price was paid, God's wrath set aside,
giving us free passage to come and abide.
The curtain was torn from the top to the floor.
Access to His presence not blocked any more.
My heart should acknowledge the gift is complete;
It's total, not part, no need to repeat.
This pass that I speak of, though it is still free,
Is totally dependent on no one but me.
Not like the others for a onetime event,
This one is diff'rent; it can never be spent.
Spent in the sense that it will never run out,
It's evidenced fully by trust and not doubt.
So back to the top, the instructions are clear;
There is one behavior that helps us draw near.
The pass for the gates and the courtyard inside,
A thankful heart ensures that we can abide.
Time after time, God's Word tells us to rejoice,
But not by command; it's hopef'ly by choice.
So to sum this all up, 'cause long-winded I'm prone,
"Thanks" is the unlimited pass to the throne.

Who Gets Offended

We often offend and aren't even aware
Of whom we offend, or maybe don't care.
When things don't go just the way that we planned,
We start to grumble, expose where we stand.
(The stance that we have is an unthankful heart;
Often tend to grumble right from the start.
We're tempted to gripe then at each little thing
That crosses our path—the stress that it brings.)
Stop for a moment and consider this thought.
It should help us think the way that we ought.
If God controls all the events of our life,
Who is it we blame when life brings us strife?
We grumble and fuss at everyone around,
Try to find someone to whom blame abounds.
We're not honest enough to go to the source;
There's no interest to challenge God, of course.
Job's wife said it well, so please hear what she said:
"Grumble at God, and you will wind up dead."
"Won't happen in this age of grace," you might say.
"God just doesn't treat His people that way."
Your statement is true and a real thankful fact;
Let me explain how I feel we react.
Let me define death as relationship lost;
Relationship strained incurs quite a cost.
Relationship, fellowship, friendship's the same,
All three are broken when grumbling's our game
I'll use this example from everyday life
That sometimes happens twixt me and my wife.
If I get upset over something she's said,
In a small way our relationship's dead.
If we don't talk, like two ships pass in the night,
Relationship's strained, and nothing is right.

It's the same with the Lord each time I complain.
I'm telling the Lord, "This trust thing's a pain."
I struggle with wanting what I think is best,
When all the Lord asks is "Trust Me and rest."
God has never been fond of the grumbling sort.
One look in His Word gives a full report.
In days long ago twelve spies entered the land,
Score ten to two, said, "Don't trust God's hand."
After the meeting they went back to their tent,
Grumbled at God, who said, "Your life's been spent."
There's another who said, "Just like God I will be."
Found he was condemned for eternity.
Today, though, it's different, yet some ways the same,
When we grumble today against God's holy name.
Death is not literal but symbolic instead;
Loss of fellowship is what we should dread.
Fellowship removed is not from God's side,
But rather from ours because of our pride.
Poetically speaking, when death's at the door,
Us setting things right need not be a chore.
With a heartfelt "I'm sorry; please forgive me;
My focus was 'me' instead of on thee,"
Lord, help me to trust you in all that you do
so my life brings glory and honor to you.
Help my heart be thankful, put grumbling aside,
That my life would have less struggle with pride.
Now Job had it right; he got right to the point:
"Is it only good that God will anoint?"
It all works for good, by Him we are told,
Agreeing with God, then peace will take hold.

Where Is the Peace?

Peace was the focus throughout the whole land,
All sick and tired of Rome's heavy hand.
Year after year, countless prophecies foretold
Of a mighty king who would fin'ly take hold.
He'd restore their kingdom like days of yore;
Their home not be occupied anymore.
So tired of waiting; 'twas no hope in sight.
Where was the peace angels promised that night?
At just the right time, the message was heard,
That night when shepherds first heard the word.
As angels arrived to spread the good news
Of peace on earth for more than just Jews.
Instead of freedom, things seemed to get worse.
God's chosen felt plagued; it must be a curse.
They sought the Lord to relieve all their plight.
Where was the peace angels promised that night?
As we look back over thousands of years,
Don't see lots of peace; instead lots of fears.
There's wars between countries, husbands, and wives,
Vi'lence is claiming just too many lives.
Mankind's heart is restless, can't settle down.
Too much of the world is wearing a frown.
It seems like this world is destined to fight.
Where is the peace angels promised that night?
Men seeking for peace, for a life of ease,
Often just freedom to do as they please.
The peace that men seek is fleeting at best.
That struggle goes on with no time to rest.
Depression, ulcers, and all kinds of strife
From lack of peace can mess up your life.

Doesn't life owe us? Isn't it our right?
Where is the peace angels promised that night?
Look at the Scripture—just what does it say?
Is there a reason peace is held at bay?
Luke says it clearly, yet oft gets left out.
No understanding will cause one to doubt.
We'd like to think that we get to decide;
It's not a given that peace will abide.
Read again carefully what those shepherds heard.
Read it slowly so you don't miss a word.
The line does not end with peace to all men;
A comma's there, not a period, my friend.
But the phrase that comes next sets up the test.
Only to those on whom "His favor" rests.
His favor resting, the qualifier's set,
But what is required that "His favor" be met?
Whoever wrote Hebrews laid it all out.
The words that God gave help eliminate doubt.
Hebrews's writer said faith is the key
to cause "His favor" rest on you and me.
Without that faith it just cannot be done.
An impossible task to please the Holy One.
So where's the peace angels promised that night?
To find that peace, look by faith, not by sight.
The fruit of faith, knowing that God's in control,
Then the trials of life will not take their toll.
Faith recognizes that God knows what's best,
Providing His kids a posture of rest.
That posture of rest gives strength to rejoice,
And that, my friend, comes only by choice.
The fruit of rejoicing, the Lord is near.
You'll find in that rest, there's no need to fear.

Not to be anxious, with thanks make requests.
You'll find with the peace of God you'll be blessed.
That peace goes beyond what you'll understand,
Will guard your heart and lead you by the hand.
As I've said before, when your peace is real,
Others around you will want what you feel.
The peace we've longed for right from the start
Won't be found without, but deep in the heart.
So when you're questioned, "Where is the peace?"
You can share with them the source of your peace.
For unto us a child was born that night,
The Savior of men to give the world light.

What a Mess—The Solution, Please

There's too much vi'lence in our land; we sit and ponder, "Why?"
If we'd just pass more stringent laws, no one would have to die.

We often get discouraged with conditions that we see.
Claim to be a Christian nation, so how could these things be?
Each time a poll is taken, most say they believe in God.
Then why is there such trouble as we walk this earthen sod?
How could this "God of Love" let all this evil still exist?
Often claim "hypocrisy" so His truths we can resist.
That quick response to judge this God as though He doesn't care,
You must know what He has said to make your judgment fair.
Gradually we've made lots of rules to put God far away.
No longer is it popular to hear what He has to say.
It actually started years ago, with fruit upon a tree
And a proclamation made: "Eat the fruit, like God you'll be."
And from that day forward that challenge has been replayed,
And man has sought for freedom from the statements God has made.
Then that quest went public, 'round nineteen sixty-two and three.
When our courts declared that schooltime prayers could no longer be.
Most people think the Bible's banned, but that's just not the case.
But if you read it publicly, they'll sure get in your face.
We've heard some teachers say there's no room for that in class.
There've been reports when students did, sometimes they did not pass.
Now public talk of God is politically incorrect.
If "I" don't want to hear it, then "my rights" you must respect.
There's now an all-out fight to get the Ten Commandments banned.
Some folks would say they have no place at all within this land.
Our courts have made decisions which have ruled that God is wrong,
And in their lofty wisdom feel there's some that don't belong.
Their arrogance was evident when they stepped across the line,
When in the case of *Roe v. Wade*, they ruled that murder's fine.

And now here not too long ago, more "wisdom" was revealed;
Our courts said it's okay to lie, the ninth of ten repealed.
That's nine of ten they've said won't stand, stand as a defense,
When used against somebody when their behavior is intense.
The tenth of ten—"don't covet"—I doubt they'll overturn,
Because "it's not what I want" that the other nine we spurn.
We're now so wise in our own eyes God's wisdom goes for naught;
We fail to pay attention and don't trust Him as we ought.

Some years ago a group of folks tried to prove that God is dead,
To justify the reason they ignore what He has said.
There are those who declare the public square is not the place;
"Talk of God should be banned; His influence must be erased."
We've made it very clear that God's not welcome in our life
Until we're faced with conflict or our life is filled with strife.
Then we call out loudly, with many tears make our appeal,
Make all kinds of promises that we're sure will seal the deal.
When God responds to our pleas and the turmoil seems to clear,
Oft forget our promise and repentance that brought Him near.
Go back to doing as before, no longer heed His call,
Then we shake our fist at God when once again we hit a wall.
How dare we shake our fist toward God and demand his presence now;
Get angry when He doesn't jump to our whens, whys, and hows?
He's done just what we've asked of Him; He's let us have our way.
But now if you wish for His reply, here's the only way.
God will respond to humble hearts, not hearts as hard as stone.
The first He'll gladly bless; the latter won't approach His throne.
Now I'll agree our land called home is really in a mess.
The answer's found in this one verse: be humble and confess.
If we would choose to seek His face and leave our ways behind,
Then He'll respond from heaven, heal our land, and peace we'll find.
He will forgive our arrogance of going our own way,
Show us how to follow Him and know peace from day to day.
Now just a word of caution, please, before this lesson ends.
What was it Jesus told us for us to be called His friends?
If we'd claim that blessed name, His commands we must obey.
To make Jesus's ways appealing, there's just no other way.
When Jesus taught us the lesson there on the grassy slope,
'Twas one spoke of a log and speck with which we all must cope.

We have a trend to shake our heads. "How could they be so blind?
If they'd give up their arrogance, they'd find that God is kind."
Before we shake our heads so hard, in pride begin to gloat,
Don't forget, without God's kindness, we'd, too, be in that boat.
Recall Jesus on the cross, prayed, "Father, they just don't know;
Please forgive them this trespass that your awesome love would show."
Ere we saw, our eyes were blind to the Way, the Truth, and Light;
'Twas by God's grace and mercy that we understand what's right.

Our prayers, like Paul's when he prayed, should be, "Lord, restore their sight.
Without the scales of blindness gone, they'll never choose what's right."
Remember it's not flesh and blood to battle with we're called,
But to stand against the spirit with which they are enthralled.
So when tempted to condemn them, be sure to face God's throne.
Your appeal: "God, show them mercy, the same that I've been shown."
And also ask for grace: "Lord, please help me show to them the same."
With this goal in mind, that they, too, would glorify your name.
One more thing before I close: go back five and twenty lines,
Way back to where 'twas mentioned "this one verse," for peace to find.
God says if our land needs healing, we've not been acting right;
We have not been careful to walk by faith and not by sight.
It's for sure this world needs changing; God's kids must show the way.
To be humble, seek forgiveness, as on our knees we pray.
Go back to acting righteously; turn from our selfish stand,
Then God'll hear from heaven, forgive our sins, and heal our land.
Remember that this God of love with tears has made appeal:
"If only you had kept My ways, your nation I would heal.
Your peace would be as a river that flows straight from My throne.
Endless grace and mercy, showing the love to which I'm prone."

The Wonder of Creation

We look at creation, the clouds in the sky,
The mountains and trees as rivers run by.
We marvel at critters that walk in the wood;
We'd fly with the birds if only we could.
Snowflakes so gorgeous; there's no two the same.
The trees in the fall with leaves all aflame;
The salmon upstream to the place of their birth.
The joy it all brings—can't value their worth.
The ice north and south and heat in between
Won't top the list of the wonders we've seen.
Everywhere we look there's beauty to behold,
For us to enjoy—by God, we are told.
The art of creation with colors ablaze,
Short contemplation is sure to amaze.
We marvel at sights; our breath goes away.
With wonder and awe, give thanks for the day.
Yet with all this beauty a problem exists:
God's best creation we often resist.
How could we resist such a glorious feat?
As we look around, it all seems complete.
The one that was made in the image of three.
Oh yes, my friend, I do mean you and me.
Too often we treat that gift with such scorn;
Too many are snuffed out before they are born.
We neglect the command "Love others too;
Consider them much more important than you."
We have little regard for such human life;
Our attitudes often cause each other strife.
Before you get pious and say "That's not me,"
Stop for a minute and listen to me.
What's held in the heart is the same as the act.
Spoken by Jesus, that statement is fact.

Our actions expose us by not showing grace,
The grace that God's given the whole human race.
When lives don't express what was done on the cross,
Creation groans, and the world's at a loss.
It's when we pick and choose who gets treated right,
The work of the cross is out of our sight.
If for no other reason than God made them so,
The grace given us to others must show.
They don't deserve it any more than do we,
But when we extend it, it's Jesus they see.
On the cross Jesus said, "They just don't know.
Father, forgive them; your mercy will show."
As we act the same, with the cross that we bear,
Then the world can believe that Jesus did care.
Though Jesus was God, grasping had no appeal;
The trip to the cross was part of the deal.
As we die daily, all creation is blessed;
Christ is exalted, and we'll be at rest.

The Spirit's Gift

Galatians 5

Do we live by the Spirit in all that we do?
Is the Spirit's "gift" operational in you?
If we look at the list that Paul laid out,
We know we too often fall short—without doubt.
It's always a challenge to look at this list,
'cause we know there are some that we've missed.
But this "gift" is diff'rent. In what way? Can you guess?
In the list Paul mentions, the "gift" has no esse.
Nine traits in Galatians, though we can't pick and choose;
Can't sort through and pick out the ones we want to use.
It's for sure we'll excel in one trait o'er the rest,
But we can't set up camp on the ones we like best.
You see that each trait Paul mentions does not stand alone,
But a part of the package that God wants to clone.
Let's start at the top—it's love Paul mentions first,
The base, the foundation of the rest of the verse.
With God's revelation of His love in our lives,
We'll find that a full and boundless joy will arise.
With love and joy blending, we'll sense freedom's release;
Freedom from fear—can now walk in confident peace.
The next five traits mentioned, some ways love's expressed;
As we live out those traits, then others will be blessed.
Now comes the tough one—to self-control is the call;
Though the end of the list, yet the hardest of all.
Most effective solution found in the next verse,
Self crucified on the cross, the end to the curse.
The curse of our self-serving life and bondage to sin,
Freedom is ours the moment the Spirit moves in.
The freedom to love and all the traits to live out,
You'll find a heart full of joy and peace but not doubt.

Now alive in the Spirit, His guidance obey,
In the Holy of Holies, with sin held at bay.
Down the page a bit farther, a caution is shown:
The harvest we reap will be exactly what's sown.
Seeds sown of the flesh, our sinful nature to feed;
Destruction will come forth in the life that we lead.
Seeds sown of the Spirit bring a much diff'rent end,
That planting's fruit will be eternal life, my friend.
However they're sown, there will be dividends,
The first in this life and then after life ends.
So let's not become weary in doing what's right.
The day's coming—we'll not walk by faith but by sight.
But till that day happens and all it will afford,
Then among the first blessings will be this reward.
With His arm 'round your shoulders and the door open wide,
"Well done, faithful servant; please come in and abide.
For your bridegroom's been waiting; now the banquet can start.
You're graciously attired, the desire of my heart."
Our reward is great, an understatement at best.
But until that day, won't know how much we're blessed.

The Quest for Peace

Eons ago a declaration was made
That peace could be known, but a price must be paid.
This world struggles for peace—elusive at best.
We all want it now, but there just is no rest.
Pretend there's a gauge in the midst of your chest.
The needle will show if you have turmoil or rest.
If the needle is stable, then peace is in play;
If the needle is moving, then it's held at bay.
Do you get uneasy if things aren't just so,
Craving the peace that you're longing to know?
When troubles arise as the day passes by,
Are there times you'd like to curl up and cry?
Are you discontent with the place that you're in?
Be careful; God considers grumbling a sin.
In the midst of the storm with the waves all around,
Could you sleep in the boat and not hear a sound
With storm waves crashing, the wind in your face?
Do you know that you've been enabled by grace?
In the midst of the fire, like three lads of old,
Would you know God's peace and walk around real bold?
Do you really want peace to reign in your life,
To rest in the calm and eliminate strife?
The answer's so simple; there's no way to hide.
This simple solution will help peace abide.
Just look to the Savior, the true Prince of Peace.
You'll see the answer for that much-sought release.
The Savior's example to sleep in the boat,
He knew that God's grace would keep it afloat.
Look at the garden, the cross, and the grave.
With joy He looked forward, this task He would brave.
He trusted His Father in every detail.
He knew that Dad's love and plans could never fail.

Brother Paul was unmoved by the things that he faced,
Knew the peace that he had could not be erased.
Beaten, imprisoned, and stoned—left for dead,
Adrift in the sea, he did not lose his head.
Paul taught, the Spirit, a bold guarantee.
God's promise that all He planned would come to be.
As we find that peace, brought by trust thru the strife,
Can help others long for a Christ-centered life.
As we find that peace grounded by trust,
As evidence to all—rejoicing's a must.
In everything give thanks; we're told to rejoice.
A thankful heart, my friend, comes only by choice.
'Twill be hard to explain to others around,
How you can feel safe, like you're on solid ground.
How you sleep in the boat without any fear,
How you always know God's presence is near.
As the world sees that fruit, peace in your life,
Your world, unshaken, as you deal with the strife.
There'll be a longing, hearts filled with desire,
That search for peace, an unquenchable fire.
Cause them to desire that much-sought release,
That's only found in the True Prince of Peace.

The Peace of God is such an amazing gift.
In moments of trial, your spirit will lift.

The Price

Would you please try to picture a balancing scale,
Those used to calculate the price of a sale.
The trays sitting even, no transaction yet;
The balance point proves a fair price will be set.
The price of salvation is placed on one tray.
The other side's for what we think we should pay.
First look at the tag, inscribed front and back;
Before you attempt, you'll know how much you lack.
Look! Both sides read zero. There's naught to be paid.
The price for salvation on Jesus was laid.
The tag placed on the tray, the standard is set;
The scale fully settled, the price must be met.
Though the paper cannot weigh more than an ounce,
The tray drops so hard that it makes the scale bounce.
But before you start to put weights on the tray
To try to determine just how much you'll pay,
An inscription engraved in the tray on the right
Can answer the question and give some insight.
"The whole universe, plus"—the words that you'll read—
Will let you know exactly how much you'll need.
With the whole universe in the tray on the right,
Since there's no "plus" to add, 'twill still be too light.
If that's still not clear enough, let me explain.
To help you from all of your efforts refrain.
It's zip, zero, nada that top off the list;
It can't be much clearer, but still we resist.
Right up front, we think it's too good to be true;
There has to be something that we pay or do.
Our pride wants to rise up, say, "See what I've done;
By my own efforts, this position I've won."
"But salvation's my gift; by faith it is free,
Not by your works lest you boast about 'me.'"

But God kindly calls us and draws us aside;
"My child, here's the price if you want to abide.
Zip, zero, nada—the bill's stamped 'Paid in Full.'
All your crimson sin will be washed white as wool.
There's only one thing that you'll have to do—
Acknowledge the fact that my Son died for you.
Though the gift is free and there are no demands,
Please would you be an extension of my hands,
For it's My desire that because of this gift,
From a pure, thankful heart your praises will lift.
And that thanksgiving is love expressed by you,
That's shown by doing all I've asked you to do.
It's not just for you, for your future's secure.
But it's also for those whose fate is unsure.
To prove you've received, you will give it away;
My love expressed through you will brighten their day.
Expressions of love, grace, compassion, and more
Will cause them to seek what I have in store.
All the treasures I have for all of mankind,
And the final account, your pure peace of mind.

The Desire for Peace

Of all of the driving forces we face,
There's one that's sought by the whole human race.
It's not food or shelter or clothing we seek,
Or savings accounts that we'd like to tweak.
Those are important, need them to exist,
Yet those are not at the top of the list.
When the votes are all in and the tally is done,
The top of the list shows peace number one.
With so much desire that peace would abound,
Must have known a time when it could be found.
For that desire to be running so deep,
There must be some hidden mem'ry we keep.
Is there a sense that goes with the main five,
Pushing and driving to keep peace alive?
Is there a gene locked in our DNA,
That causes us to look for peace that way?
Let's look back through hist'ry, the record's clean;
Just find one entry where true peace is seen.
In a garden cool, we walked all day.
In the evening breeze the trees would sway.
All the animals there, just like a pet,
Did not run and hide—no fear of man yet.
Fruit hung on the trees, 'twas plenty of food,
All contributing to that peaceful mood.
All those were factors, but what made the scene,
We had fellowship with the Hand Unseen.
The Hand Unseen, as the Creator is known,
His only desire that His love be shown.
Yet that sweet taste planted so deep within
Was still not enough to keep us from sin.
We chose to rebel; we had it so good.
Chose not to behave the way that we should.

'Twas only one rule, that peace to retain,
Now "Woe unto me" is our sad refrain.
That peace now shattered is Paradise Lost;
Our want to regain, we'd pay any cost.
It can't be purchased, just too high a fee;
Yet that fee was paid that day on the tree.
We search all day long; we clamor for peace,
But try as we might, the struggle won't cease.
The classrooms are full; the world tries to teach,
But that peace is always just out of reach.
We come to the table of peace we'd talk;
If the table's not right, we threaten to walk.
One silly choice o'er which we choose to fight;
Talks won't even start if seating's not right.
Even when treaties are signed, they don't last;
Too often the parties can't forgive the past.
Peace so elusive, filled with despair,
Almost sure peace will never be there.
But looking ahead a ways down the road,
Here's a report that should lighten your load.
That peace that we crave, for which we've implored,
Paradise Lost will one day be restored.
There's only one place true peace will abide.
It's the land where the Prince of Peace resides.
There will be a day in that land we can know;
The peace spoken of so long, long ago.
"Peace to all men on whom His favor rests."
Now saints through the ages eternally blessed.
The King of Kings rises—plan's now complete;
Those whom He's chosen will sit at His feet.
But till that day, we'll see turmoil and strife;
All kinds of things try to mess up our life.
A proper perspective will bring peace near,
In midst of turmoil, eliminate fear.

That peace will surpass what we comprehend,
As we can trust Him in all things, my friend.
There's no circumstance—He's not caught off guard—
That God cannot use, no matter how hard.
To bring His will about, He will not fail.
In peace, all attacks will never prevail.
He's promised in all the tests that we face
The strength to go through, provided by grace.
The grace that shows us He knows what's best.
Helps us be peaceful, in His glory rest.
Life's like a play that we must watch unfold,
And we know the end—His glory gets told.
Knowing the end, that the vict'ry is sure,
A peace can be ours till hope is secure.
Time after time this thought has been spoken.
When we're at peace, it's more than a token.
The world'll take notice, for they crave it too.
The quiz will be, "How can I be like you?"
Then hearts are open; they're ready to hear.
The truth can be shared that brings Jesus near.

Suggestions for a Godly Marriage

As you start your life together, there'll be lessons you must learn.
That challenges will test you at each corner that you turn.
There are some crucial factors that you have to keep in mind
When dealing with your new spouse and the peace you want to find.
Paul tells us in Ephesians, "It's God's armor that we need."
For going into battle, God's protection we must plead.
The breastplate and the helmet, plus the shield, the belt, and shoes.
And the Sword of the Spirit, we're told, we must always use.
These weapons are not carnal but divinely energized
To help us with our struggles till our hope is realized.
With all the armor listed, it seems there is a lack.
The body's mostly covered, yet there's no armor for the back.
I know at least two reasons that the back can be revealed.
One reason there is listed; the second is more concealed.
We're told, now dressed in armor, we're to stand and never run.
Standing with the Shield of Faith will bring glory to the Son.
The second, though, is hidden, clearly stated nonetheless.
I'm told to watch your backside; "it's others you must bless."
Now to tie this all together for a husband and a wife—
One secret to hold on to as you start this brand-new life.
Please purpose with each other when you're tempted to attack.
Never standing toe to toe; instead, always back to back.
In a stance of back to back, you will find it's hard to fight.
It's then you'll be reminded that fighting isn't right.
Every fight that's ever been in the history of mankind,
The root of every conflict has been "Not your will but mine."
Though equals in God's kingdom, you each have a separate role.
Don't lord o'er each other; don't let pride exact a toll.

Please don't forget, dear brother, the command to love your wife.
For you it's not an option, but the pattern for your life.

Commanded then to love her, just like Jesus loved his bride.
He laid His life down freely; for His bride He gladly died.
Remember, this dear lady, that God chose for you this man,
To provide for, to defend you, and to lead you by the hand.
The Word tells you be willing, submissively show respect;
That together with His love, your marriage will perfect.
It is love to give protection to watch each other's back.
For when a back's not covered, then the enemy will attack.
For it's not with flesh and blood that the battle should be fought,
So keep your struggle focused on the enemy as you ought.
The preacher taught in Proverbs through relationships God planned;
A life can be clearly changed with love and a gentle hand.
As iron sharpens iron, by each other we're refined,
The mate that God has given—the best "tool" He had in mind.
When tools, behaving rightly, help complete God's planned design;
Remove traits not of the Spirit—can hone and help refine.
Now both of you remember the pattern God has in mind;
You two can become as one, then love and peace you'll find.
The biggest test you will face is to set yourself aside.
Encouraging each other, you'll find true love will abide.
So again this silly phrase, "When tempted to attack,
Be sure to change your posture; make the battle back to back."
For when the battle's over and the foe is on the run,
Then the time for toe to toe you'll find 'twill be more fun.
So pledge to one another your love will remain ever pure.
As God knits you together, that pledge will be locked and secure.
God bless you both!

Search for Messiah

Unsettled at best, this world that we're in,
The peace of the garden, shattered by sin.
That day when Adam stepped out of place,
Affected, my friend, the whole human race.
This world's been troubled for so many years;
We've longed for Messiah, sought Him with tears.
We've studied hard, all the Scriptures of old,
And made lists of signs as they were foretold.
Throughout the years, Messiah's been sought,
Though often mistaken—they all went for naught.
When things were good, they thought He'd come,
"Our hope's fulfilled!" was the thinking of some.
But when things looked bleak and all seemed for naught,
Then once again, Messiah they sought.
Their search for Messiah, promised of old,
They checked off the list as they were foretold.
They knew the prophecies, knew well the list.
They'd just seen them all; nothing was missed.
Though right in their midst, chose not to rejoice,
A suffering Messiah was not their first choice.
The Messiah sought for, right off "their list";
He'd clean up their home with a hard iron fist.
Threatened by teachings they'd not want to hear,
Shook their whole world, loss of pow'r brought fear.
Fear led to anger, then anger to hate,
That hate called for death; they just couldn't wait.
Hatred so bitter, judged He should die,
One of their own gave the one reason why:
"It's better that one die than all of the rest."
He didn't know why; the Spirit knew best.
Blinded by hate, they just refused to see
All the signs foretold had just come to be.

Hatred so clouded their vision, you say,
satan stirred the pot, thought 'twas his day.
Even that hatred was part of God's plan,
The day God's love met the hatred of man.
Scripture proclaims that love's greatest form,
One dies for another; it's just not the norm.
Jesus displayed that great love on the cross;
Considered pure joy, 'twas not thought a loss.
Rejected and beaten—the hatred did show.
"Father, forgive them, they just didn't know."
Tortured and abused till death had its way.
But what a surprise came on the third day.
The grave could not hold him; death lost its sting.
Came forth in vict'ry, was crowned King of Kings.
The final sign was now checked off the list.
Still no acceptance, the blessing they missed.
Why were they so stubborn and oh so blind?
The Messiah they sought, they would not find.
Please be sure, my friend, we don't act the same,
To go our own way, rejecting his name.
We too quickly judge—"How blind could they be?"
But look real close; you might see you and me.
We, too, have ideas of how things should be.
Hold on real tight when it challenges me.
Challenged to surrender, let go and trust,
To walk as Christian, my friend—it's a must.
Just as Christ suffered, we will suffer too.
He laid down His life; that's required of you.
No longer our own, been bought with a price;
Total surrender will honor that price.
When asked to surrender, we should obey.
Without the filter, "I'll do it my way."
Look in the throne room—there's only one chair.
Just where will you sit if Jesus sits there?

I dare you to tell Him, "Give me the chair.
I think I know better; I should sit there."
Arrogant, foolish, we'd never do that!
Be honest for once—that's right where we're at.
When we make our plans, ignore what God's said.
We're arrogant fools, with so much to dread.
When we make our plans, ignore God's advice,
We'll find that our stance is on real thin ice.
We should humble ourselves, vacate the throne,
Give God His place that His glory be shown.

Creation and the Choice

We take so much for granted, lose the awesomeness of God.
We don't bother being thankful as we walk this earthen sod.
With everything around us made by His almighty hand,
There's nothing without order; He holds all things in His hand.
The trees we see before us, all the mountains and the streams
Are made for our enjoyment; they're more beautiful than dreams.
He keeps the planets spinning, all the stars are held in place,
The moon with all its splendor—they're just never out of place.
From the greatest to the smallest creatures found upon the earth,
Too often we don't ponder or consider what they're worth.
Without the tilt on axis, the seasons just would not be,
And this life we love so much, my friend, it just would not be.
With all things held together, suspended and held in place.
It's not by ropes and wires but by His amazing grace.
That great sustaining power, if we but take the time to look,
Is found between the covers, written in God's holy book.
It's all laid out before us and just why He cares so much.
In all things He's created, He displays His awesome touch.
He tells us we're created in the image of this God,
Wanting to have fellowship so that we can walk with God.
But there's a wall between this God and His creation.
The self-expressed rebellion leaves us with consternation.
The consternation grips us; there's naught that we can do.
Rebellion overwhelms us; it's our nature thru and thru.
But then this God of mercy with expressions of His grace
Made His Son a sacrifice to redeem the human race.
The plan's been set before us; now the choice is ours to make.
We have the information; choose the path that we should take.
Accepting God's provision He's provided thru His Son,
The gift of grace and mercy makes us co-heirs with the Son.
The choice will be eternal, for God has declared it so.
Make the choice whom you will serve and which way you want to go.

Communion, Then Service

The last time He ate it,
There were twelve others there.
He broke bread and blessed it
And encouraged them there.

"I will not eat again
Of this bread or this cup
Till the next time we share
At the famed marriage sup."

He said, "I am going,
But someday I'll return.
Now we'll send the Spirit;
The truth you will learn.

"But before I leave you,
Let me show you one thing:
I'll be washing your feet.
You'll be served by your King.

"Now do unto others
As I've done for you,
By serving your brothers
In all that you do.

"The service is giving
Of your time and your life.
In service to others
At a cost to your life.

"Remembrance is doing
All the things I have done.
Your service to others
Mirrors the life of the Son."

Choices

Flee from youthful lust, my friend; be quick to run away.
Don't stick around to find out if sin will rule the day.

Often we don't run away as quickly as we ought.
Our flesh just wants to linger but avoid being caught.

We think God will give the strength, allowing us to stand
And let our flesh get "tickled" as we try to make that stand.

The strength He gives ain't to stand; instead it's just to run,
To flee the things we should avoid, even if they're "fun."

Should be the Spirit's guidance that tells us when to turn
And flee the situations, the sins that we should spurn.

The training that allows us to hear the Spirit's voice
Is knowing what God's word says, to help us make our choice.

In several ways, God tells us how to avoid getting caught,
To run, abstain, and to flee, and act just as we ought.

Don't do what the wicked do; bad company isn't good.
Even avoid appearances of things we never should.

All of these suggestions are not to take away our fun,
But give us clues to live the life pleasing to the Son.

So avoid the things we should not do; quickly turn and run.
Keep your witness spotless—an example of the Son.

Blessings and Guidance

The Lord knows how to bless us with exactly what we need.
Each and every passing day, we'll have no want or need.
If we'll but seek to serve Him and seek His kingdom first,
the daily needs will follow, the second aft the first.
Sometimes we find that many things don't go the way we planned,
and then we have to seek to know just how God has things planned.
Many times no answer comes, and we have to walk by faith.
Trust the Lord to do it right; don't give up—don't doubt your faith.
If we can just give up the right to choose which way we go
and follow God's eternal plan, He'll show which way to go.
The hardest thing we'll ever do is set aside the right
to have the final word to say for us which way is right.
There is a choice we have to make and make it every day,
to cling to what the Lord God says for guidance for the day.
Many times it's very hard to follow after God,
because we can't see up ahead; we lack in trusting God.
Man will never understand or know the mind of God,
allowing man to look ahead, thus never needing God.
God has a plan for all of us. It's found in Christ the Son.
Regardless what we think or say, God says it's thru His Son.
There is no other way to go, no matter what we say.
The only way is thru the Son of God; He has the final say.
If we look into the Word, we'll find that Jesus wins;
Accept the work of Jesus's blood, find victory over sin.

Blessed Is the One . . .

Look to the lesson Christ taught on the mount.
He taught a list of the blessings that count.
Poor in spirit at the top of the list;
Read them all down so that nothing gets missed.
Poor in spirit, I'm aware of my plight;
Without God's help, life will never be right.
Those who mourn will have a repentant heart.
The comfort comes, bringing a new start.
The next calls for gentle, sometimes called meek;
Strength under control—the earth they don't seek.
For those who hunger to do what is right,
Satisfaction will be there within sight.
To those who show mercy and not hold back,
They too shall receive, of mercy no lack.
The pure in heart, those free of self's fire,
Will walk by sight with the God they desire.
Those who make peace while walking this sod
Will be known by all as the sons of God.
Those who get beat up for doing what's right,
For them heaven's kingdom is now in sight.
For those who are hated, the subject of lies,
You're hated because they see Christ in your eyes.
Rejoice and be glad; you won't be alone.
Others were hated en route to God's throne.
You'll be in good comp'ny; the Master's there too.
Hatred toward Him will be transferred to you.
Don't give up hope when faced with things tough.
His faithful promise: "My grace is enough."
With this being stated, might not understand.
Please rest assured, He has it all in hand.
Of the list Christ taught, not just things to do,
But rather Christ's nature revealed in you.

As we surrender, put self on the cross,
Then God's favor will reverse any loss.
Not that He'll give back what's taken away;
Instead, just His peace to get thru each day.
To know that peace is much better than gold,
To walk with Him, more than riches untold.
The things of this earth will soon pass way,
But the light of His glory—oh what a day!

Alone? Never!

Inspired by a devotion in *Our Daily Bread*

An Indian lad, as legend goes, sent to the woods alone,
From dusk to dawn throughout the night, his courage would be shown.
The sounds throughout the woods that night, unsettling at best,
Kept sleep from coming to his eyes; was hard to stop and rest.
Felt sure that he was all alone still set to make his stand;
Was unaware that he was watched by tender loving hands.
He kept a fire burning bright to keep predators at bay;
He struggled hard to keep it fed until the break of day.
As morning broke, the lad awoke, rubbed sleep out of his eyes;
There stood a silhouetted form against the morning skies.
Blinked again and rubbed his eyes, could not fathom what he saw;
He recognized the silhouette—it was his own grandpa.
He ran into his warm embrace, tears streaming from his eyes;
Then he realized the fears he felt were nothing but big lies.
Aware he'd been protected by love of a special kind
Immediately brought comfort to ease his troubled mind.
Reflecting on the night gone by, a question came to mind:
If I had known Grandpa was there, would fear be hard to find?
We're oft just like that Indian lad when sure we're all alone;
Will struggle with those fearful thoughts to which we're often prone.
But oh, dear friend, please ne'er forget, He's promised to be near,
And basking in His perfect love will always drive out fear.
Scripture says that love gives us faith and hope through any test;
The promise comes to us by love because it is the best.

Adopted as Sons

Still the story goes on
in the court of the King.
Another offender
now a child of the King.

Our nature's offensive
just because of our sins.
And heaven's off limits;
there's just no place for sin.

At just the right time,
when the season was right,
the Father sent His Son;
had Him set all things right.

He met the requirements
to redeem from the law.
Set relationships right;
now we're free from the law.

With relationships new,
His Spirit says we're sons,
Crying, "Abba Father,"
we're adopted as sons.

We're no longer orphans.
We're a part of the clan,
wanted as children,
God's completed plan.

As a part of the clan,
we're listed as heirs.
The inheritance ours,
with Christ we are heirs.

Acts of Kindness

A simple act of kindness,
a giant statement made,
could help someone understand
salvation's price was paid.

Our simple acts speak volumes
of sacrifices made.
Setting plans of self aside,
someone's day's been made.

The act of blessing others
speaks of the Savior's love.
Who gave His life in service
to Father's love above.

He laid his life down freely
to die for you and me,
showing us the greatest love
the world would ever see.

Greater love has no man seen
than for a man to die
in service to another life
so the other might not die.

Jesus died upon that tree
in place of you and me.
He spent his life's blood freely
that death we might not see.

When we do those little things
in service to another,
that selfless act speaks volumes
of love for one another.

Don't think light of service done
no matter what the size.
It might be the act of love
that opens up their eyes.

Absolutes

We really don't like them, and I'll tell you why.
When things are all settled, there's no room for "I."

"I" wants the last chance to say what is right,
But if there's resistance, I'm ready to fight.

Every battle that started in the history of man
Goes back to the feeling "You're wrong; I'm the man."

"I will have my rights," we all seem to say.
No matter what happens, we want our own way.

What's important to you means nothing to me,
because I have chosen to please only me.

Since both sides are stubborn and won't give an inch,
We both need someone to break up the clinch.

So Jesus steps in and draws us aside
and asks us, each one, "Put away all your pride."

It was pride that started this conflict in motion.
Set aside all pride and stop the commotion.

To find peaceful living, I have a plan.
It's really quite simple: "Serve your fellow man."

Absolutes? Ha!

Absolutes? Ha! The whole world would say
I have the right to choose my own way.
No one can tell me what I should do,
If there's a God, then not even you.
I'll be my own god, even my king.
Make my own choices, do my own thing.
Don't tell me I must give up my will,
To think of others—oh, what a thrill.
I know it all and what's best for me.
What's all this talk? Who died on a tree?
Who needs a savior? I'm doing fine.
Who needs a savior? Who says that I'm lost?
Life must please me, no matter the cost.
Absolutes listed—if I don't agree,
What does it mean for someone like me?
Someone who thinks, "I'll do my own thing."
If I'm wrong, what does my future bring?"
God says, "My friend, there's only one way.
I have called you, so please don't delay.
I am the Way, the Truth, and the Life."
Response, my friend, can bring you new life.
"I am the Way"; the choice must be made,
Heaven or hell, the price has been paid.
Yes or no, you will have to decide
If with the Savior you want to abide.
Choose your own way; the outcome is set.
The price for your sins just can't be met.
"It's a free gift; I've called you each one.
My will's you all would live with the Son."

A Plan to Redeem

Ere the clock started ticking,
God had a plan.
A plan to redeem
each lost, sinful man.

Sinful? Yes, sinful,
with a heart made of stone.
So blood must be shed
our sins to atone.

The blood must be innocent,
perfect, clean without spot,
obeying every law,
every tittle and jot.

"But, God, I can't do it;
it just can't be done."
"I know," said the Father,
"so I'll send my Son.

"His blood will be innocent,
both perfect and clean,
and if washed in His blood,
your sins won't be seen.

"With your sins now covered,
what's left to atone?
The greeting's still open;
ascend to my throne.

"Come into my presence
and spend time with me.
I will love you, my child,
for eternity."

The Rose

Retelling of a sermon set to rhyme

The date had been set; the church took a chance
To talk to their kids, what they think is romance.
Why kids should stay pure was the topic that day.
Hoping to teach them to behave the right way.
As the kids filed in, all the lights were down low.
Spotlight on the stage, giving off a soft glow.
A lone, single rose in a vase on the stage
The speaker removed, as he turned the first page.
He handed it off at the start of the row;
Said, "Please pass it on; object lesson will show."
The rose made its rounds as the lecture went on,
For each to admire and to then pass it on.
From hand to hand passed, the rose went down each row.
The toll on the rose was beginning to show.
The stem was now bent, all the leaves damaged too.
The petals now wilted, there remained just a few.
Lecture completed, the rose back in the vase.
Diff'rent expressions are now etched on each face.
Some kids looked troubled; realized what they'd done.
While some others looked smug—thought they were better than some.
That thing of beauty, as he'd started his speech
Looked like some refuse that washed up on the beach.
Now any appeal that had been there before,
The damage was done; that rose wanted no more.
Then after a moment, the speaker arose.
Asked them this question: "Now would you want this rose?"
They all shook their heads, for they all understood,
That now that old rose, it was damaged—no good.
After discussions, they got up to depart.
Something strange happened that would change every heart.

Remember Daniel and the hand at the wall?
A message was scribed in the great banquet hall.
Lecture hall silent, saw a hand at the wall.
'Twas a nail scared hand; wrote red letters real tall.
"I still want that rose!
I died for that rose!"

No need to expound, for the message was clear.
True love covers all; restoration's so dear.

ORDER INFORMATION

To order additional copies of this book, please visit
www.redemption-press.com.
Also available at Amazon, Christian bookstores,
and Barnes and Noble.

CPSIA information can be obtained
at www.ICGtesting.com
Printed in the USA
JSHW051143120523
41613JS00002B/10